BBC MUSIC GUIDES

Brahms Chamber Music

IVOR KEYS

BRITISH BROADCASTING CORPORATION

Contents

Published by the British Broadcasting Corporation
35 Marylebone High Street, London W1M 4AA
ISBN 0 563 10168 7
First published 1974
Reprinted 1978
© Ivor Keys 1974
Printed in England by The Whitefriars Press Ltd,
London and Tonbridge

TON SIXTH FORM COLL

BRAHMS CHAMBER MUSIC

Contradictions

Schoenberg, of all people, devoted a lengthy chapter to Brahms in *Style and Idea* called 'Brahms the Progressive', and paid him the eccentric homage of orchestrating his Piano Quartet, Op. 25. Cecil Gray, on the other hand, seemed in 1927 to be trying to resuscitate the nearly lifeless corpse of Brahms's reputation by using the kiss of death – writing off most of the large-scale music and salvaging the songs and piano miniatures. Party battle-cries – in a battle not of Brahms's instigation – have resounded ever since Bülow's ridiculous formula of the three Bs – Bach, Beethoven, Brahms – whose alliteration purports to put Brahms above Mozart, and whose longevity has prevented the adoption of the alternative trinity of Berlioz, Bruckner and Bartók. But whilst the adulation (now somewhat defensive) and detraction continue in critical circles, sometimes in terms as divorced from objectivity as anything Berlioz used to suffer, the fact can be attested in concert-giving societies up and down the country that a higher proportion of the total works of Brahms is regularly performed than of any other composer except perhaps Beethoven. We take Brahms's repertoire for granted, and some of us may well resent its use in chamber music clubs as a 'modern' alternative to the Viennese classics. H. C. Colles, taken literally, might be exaggerating in suggesting[1] that but for Brahms the nineteenth century might have seen, and indeed deliberately encompassed, the death of the extended chamber work; yet looking at the contributions, if any, of other great figures such as Berlioz, Schumann, Liszt, Wagner and even the relatively prolific Mendelssohn, we can see what Colles means. With the tide of new music running so strongly in directions which seemed to prove that the day of pure chamber music was over and that its revival was a treacherous and futile exercise in archaeology, the achievement of such works as Brahms's two first piano quartets was a very real one. To add to such achievements year by year in the face of convincing master-pieces of totally different forms and genres such as Liszt's *Faust* Symphony or his piano sonata was a work of passionate intellectual integrity. It would have been far easier (it may well be the same case today) to join those who were uncritically blazing trails in all directions than to continue on a broader highway,

[1] In *The Chamber Music of Brahms* (Musical Pilgrim Series, OUP, 1933).

well surfaced and lit, and to send his own traffic along it, ready for road testing and abhorring camouflage.

The consciousness of a mighty musical heritage haunted Brahms ever since the tremendous public salute with which Schumann hailed him in 1853. Twenty years previously Schumann had founded a magazine called *Neue Zeitschrift für Musik* as a platform for the expression of the new Romanticism which seemed to him and to other ardent young spirits to be urgently necessary. The Davids who in the early numbers helped sling verbal stones against the Philistines included such figures as Mendelssohn, Wagner and Heller, all members of a guerrilla band of Schumann's imagining called the Davidsbündler. Although by 1853 the magazine was in other hands Schumann, with characteristic generosity and liveliness of expression, contributed an article called 'Neue Bahnen' (New Paths) which included phrases like these about the virtually unknown visitor from Hamburg:

I felt . . . that one day there must suddenly emerge the one who would be chosen to express the most exalted spirit of the times in an ideal manner, one who would not bring us mastery in gradual developmental stages but who, like Minerva, would spring fully armed from the head of Jove. And he has arrived . . . his name is Johannes Brahms.

Schumann goes on to mention 'sonatas, or rather veiled symphonies', songs, individual piano pieces, sonatas for violin and piano, and string quartets. Certainly nothing survives of this date from the last two categories; these works must have been victims of the exacting self-criticism induced by so tremendous a public introduction. Inevitable and understandable as were the inhibitions caused by the great shadows of the classical forbears – even in the full maturity of 1877 Brahms was to recoil at Bülow calling the first symphony 'the Tenth' – there is a certain irony in the situation. That Schumann was a great and perceptive critic no one who has read his essay on Berlioz's *Fantastic* Symphony – astonishingly, done from a piano arrangement – can deny. But his language towards Brahms in 'Neue Bahnen' brims with Romanticism: 'We were drawn into a circle of ever-growing magic. . . . He, like a thundering stream, would unite all into a waterfall, bearing a rainbow over the rushing waves, met on the shore by fluttering butterflies, and accompanied by the voices of nightingales.' And although to us the most notable feature of the

opening of Brahms's piano sonata in C, Op. 1 – doubtless one of
the pieces with which he astonished Schumann and his friends – is
a barn-storming reminiscence of a 'classic' (Beethoven's *Hammerklavier* Sonata, Op. 106), all three early piano sonatas are full of
'Davidsbündler' qualities – flamboyant Romantic gestures, and
even a folk-song quotation with a refrain about the beloved blue
flower – which must have convinced Schumann that Brahms was
'one of them'. When some early works were published as a result
of Schumann's article Brahms wrote to him: 'I still cannot get
used to seeing these innocent children of nature in such decent
clothing.' Brahms is already standing back in cool appraisal. The
relentless and fascinating way in which he tidied up in later life
the first surviving child of nature among the chamber works –
the Trio in B, Op. 8 – is a documented example of a process which
went on incessantly, and the somewhat detailed discussion of its
two versions in chapter four is an attempt to show some of the
ways in which he might have become more truly 'one of them'
had he not been Johannes Brahms. By 'decent clothing' he
doubtless originally meant simply the dignity of being in print.
But the 'decent clothing' of his ideas came to mean far more: not
a prudish hiding of nakedness but a balance, powerful because
poised, between what is said and how it is said – the ideal being
that the expression should be so perfect that it is impossible to
separate matter from manner. The struggle for equilibrium
between variety and coherence, between the scope of the ideas
and the length of time taken to present them – this struggle makes
the composition of each piece a new battleground where the
issues are fought out. Brahms's battles are watched over by
heroes of the past who had fought and won them, and we know
that the field was littered with the corpses of his uncompleted or
destroyed compositions.

The effect of this unseasonable maturity is that in the chamber
works it is impossible to speak dogmatically of a progression from
stylistically early works through a middle of increasing maturity
to an Olympian end. The impression is rather one which Brahms
doubtless strove to make – and not merely out of deference to
Schumann – of Minerva springing fully armed from the head of
Jove. This doesn't mean that a survey of the chamber music is an
inevitable reverential paean. The new wine doesn't always suit
the old bottles and is sometimes musty when poured. Some of it

is flat, some is undeniably thick. But it does mean that except for the Indian summer of the late works involving the clarinet the rest of the chamber music is best divided by categories (corresponding to the Breitkopf and Härtel complete edition) rather than by chronology. This book may thus best serve its primary purpose as a listener's handbook, and there is an index for the purpose; but it also aims to be readable straight through, for Brahms's methods usually involved the systematic consolidation of newly-won territories by at least a pair of examples in quick succession.

In tending towards larger ensembles in his earlier chamber works, Brahms followed his natural bent and delayed invidious comparisons. (An apparent exception, the Trio, Op. 8, has markedly 'non-classical' features in its earlier form.) His delight in rich sonorities led to the string sextets; his mastery as a pianist led to the piano quartets and the piano quintet. The latter is considered first and in some detail because its first movement offers examples of his constructive methods which are convenient to print. It doesn't have pride of place for any other reason. The listener who can neither read the staff notation nor get a friend to play for him can rest assured that its incidence thereafter decreases sharply for reasons of space and economics.

The Pianoforte Quintet and the Pianoforte Quartets

QUINTET FOR PIANO AND STRING QUARTET IN F MINOR, OP. 34

Allegro non troppo: Andante, un poco adagio: Scherzo & Trio: Allegro non troppo.

Brahms originally wrote this as a string quintet. He repudiated this version, published it as a sonata for two pianos and finally (1865) published it as a piano quintet. A close look at the opening shows clearly how Brahms is able to make his materials change and grow before the mind's ear and yet retain a reassuring coherence. The reader without the patience or resources to trace the melodic analysis through these six examples may yet find them useful, since taken in succession they give a résumé of the exposition, though the work's richness makes it a far from exhaustive one. Brahms begins thus:

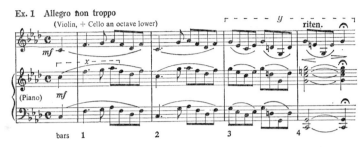

If so early a pause is not to have a tentative effect, it must be pregnant, not languishing. The energy bursts out thus:

But totally new material might make the opening sound like a false start. The first four semiquavers in Ex. 2 take their shape from the first four notes of the theme, those in bar 5 from the strings in bars 3 and 4 (see the brackets *x* and *y* respectively). The rhythm of Ex. 2 has a typical dislocation, the silences being contrived to throw the accents half a bar away from their original position. Even the first violin's falling semitone (*z*) will turn out to be grist to the mill. Here it is marked with accents at the end of the first, already varied, reprise (bars 12 ff.):

Ex.3

(Violins, + Viola and Cello an octave lower)

Here again, a bar later, it has become a connecting tissue, and the erstwhile *theme*, in its semiquaver shape, has become an *accompaniment* (see the bracketed *x y*):

Ex. 4

At bar 23 the tail of Ex. 3 has become the head of a 'new' theme (what indeed *is* 'new' in this context?):

Ex. 5

At bar 57 the plangent tones of the viola vary *this* theme and the semiquavers recur:

Ex. 6
(Viola & Cello)

It is notable how far and how quickly the tonality has shifted. The key signature of Ex. 6 now contains four sharps instead of four flats. This new key (C sharp minor) has been in force, though even then with several temporary deviations, since the drop to the work's first *pianissimo* marking the start of the second subject paragraph. One could argue that at Ex. 6 we are temporarily in F sharp minor. Be that as it may, whether we are talking of C sharp (a semitone away from the home key's dominant, C) or of F sharp (a semitone from the home tonic of F) we must realise that whilst the *notes* are physically close to each other their *keys* (in the sense of tonality) are not near relatives at all. This effect of stepping into a surprisingly distant realm has a mystery all its own. But it transpires that it is no mere whimsicality, for in the recapitulation we have the first subject, in F minor, *forte* after a hesitant start, followed by a *pianissimo* F *sharp* minor for the re-entry of the second subject, which slips magically back down the semitone to F minor when for the first time in the work (at the 208th bar!) the string quartet is heard alone. Then, if not before, it is borne in on us, subconsciously or otherwise, that this descending semitone, which may have meant little or nothing in Ex. 2, is the principal thread of coherence in the whole movement.

These processes, fascinating though they may be, cannot in themselves make a masterpiece. If the original ideas are not good enough the manipulation has a fabricated air – some might think this movement's development not free from that charge. But this doesn't alter the fact that no extended instrumental composition can ever be convincing if it doesn't possess the coherence that comes from integrity. But lest the reader should feel that he has seen more trees than wood it should be pointed out that these technical means serve a simple, carefully balanced emotional design. The two main subject-paragraphs, one loud, the other mainly soft, are both based in minor keys, enhancing the effect of a consolatory gleam of major in the last moments of the exposition. The development is by and large an interrupted *crescendo* from indeterminate languor to *fortissimo* passion. The recapitulation is still insistent on the minor keys until a parallel 'relenting' to that of the exposition. Then a slower tempo and a passage of unaccompanied string quartet presage a happy ending, which is suddenly thrust aside in a vehement reversion to the storms of the opening minor.

The tensions have quite departed from the slow movement, which has a very similar 'feel' to that which Brahms calls 'Romanze' in the C minor String Quartet. It is easy-going in three respects – it has a simple ABA shape in which the reprise is luxuriously rescored rather than rethought; there is little avoidance of the standard four-bar length of the phrases, whose regularity is indeed emphasised by the constant recurrence of the rhythm and shape of the tune's first bar; and the harmony deals in thirds and sixths in more than a hundred of the 126 bars, which is indulgent even for Brahms. The oscillating semitone re-enters momentarily (bars 113–15) to cause the final climax by a gleaming modulation.

Over a *pizzicato* pulse on the bottom note of the cello it seems as though the scherzo is to inhabit the same shadowy C minor world of the corresponding movements in Opp. 25, 87 or 101. But the syncopated *pianissimo* opening in 6/8 time first turns into a 2/4 march, Ex. 7(*a*), which in turn is suddenly broken into by a *fortissimo* chordal 6/8 passage, Ex. 7 (*b*); there is no transition – the obvious thematic connection being sufficient. (Talking of thematic connections, note the very close one between Ex. 7(*a*) and the first two bars of Ex. 5.)

There is nothing conventional about the order and the keys in which these three elements occur. There are abrupt changes of dynamics, and in one of the softer passages Ex. 7(*a*) is given an erudite fugal treatment with three counter-subjects, one of which seems to be referred to in the middle of the succeeding 'Trio'. But the most impressive passages are the 'hammer and tongs'

Ex. 7(a)

ones, and the main limb of the scherzo carries to the limits of emphasis a D flat → C cadence (our falling semitone yet again, or perhaps rather Schubert's in this case, from the end of the C major Quintet). In this connection it is interesting to note that the suppressed string quintet version of the work used, like Schubert, two cellos rather than two violas. For Trio we launch into a 'noble' diatonic tune which is with Brahms a frequent form of heavy relief at such places.

The finale begins with an extended chromatic groping, with the initial counterpoint dwelling on ambiguities and with a rising semitone much in evidence. The eventual transition is not from darkness to light but to a theme still in the minor, given initially to the cello and marked *tranquillo* – a paradoxical marking for a tune hovering between the plaintive and the whimsical, which is characteristic of Brahms when he is determined not to be ebullient. It is characteristic too of a certain tone of the cello's voice, and its *locus classicus* is the beginning of the last movement of the Double Concerto for violin, cello and orchestra, Op. 102. For some of its course this movement does not seem so tautly constructed; the transitions seem rather abrupt, and the themes and their variants have the air of random bedfellows. But this impression may have been intended, for in the long coda at which we at last get a *presto* (but still *non troppo*) Brahms pulls the threads together with real energy. After some fifty bars come *fortissimo* tonic chords which could well mark the end of the piece. Instead we swerve aside to a loud statement of the hitherto undramatic second subject. Again we seem to hear terminal noises, but again the second subject supervenes, gradually losing its impulse after wide modulation. After a pause we hark back to the syncopations of the scherzo, and the music explodes into a final drastic epigram.

The sustained energy of this close is not common in Brahms and seemed uncharacteristic to his closest friends, whose opinions he often sought in true humbleness and sometimes, it seems, in real perplexity. But here, as usual, he let his first thoughts stand, presumably because a truncated *presto* would not balance the long introduction – and one prizes the uninhibited gallop when at last it breaks through.

PIANO QUARTET NO. 1 IN G MINOR, OP. 25

Allegro: Intermezzo (Allegro, ma non troppo) and Trio (Animato): Andante con moto: Rondo alla Zingarese (Presto).
Composed 1857/61. Published 1863.

The first movement raises acutely the tension between 'innocent children of nature' and 'decent clothing'. What a lot there is to admire in the sure-footed variety and surprise of the transient modulations, and in the integrity and disciplined certainty of the long-range tonal planning! It is hard to imagine any of Brahms's contemporaries in mid-century having the musical intelligence to perceive and borrow such resources from analysis of their Viennese forbears – or even considering such analysis to be relevant or worthwhile. To take one example on the credit side: the first subject, as with so many of Mozart's, poses two quite different statements or limbs, the first in angular unison (compare Mozart's String Quartet K.428 in E flat) and the second in sweet chordal dialogue, not continuing in the same minor key, but indulging a Schubert-like plunge into a new key whose effect is heightened by a preceding silence (Ex. 8, opposite).

This classical dualism enables two formal effects to be made: after a spacious exposition the literal repetition of the ten bars of the first limb makes us wonder whether a repeat is being made, and this increases our interest when a quite different key for the second limb shows we are after all on a new path; and the recapitulation proper is made not by the first but by the second limb, quietly gleaming in the tonic major. This key, not otherwise heard till the 155th bar of the last movement, has here the effect of a patch of blue sky before the minor key obliterates it again. Yet whilst one admires, with Schoenberg, the control of the

Ex. 8 (i)

(ii)

materials (and the self-control it implies), the calculated balance, and the 'seamless' coherence of the motivic work in the transitions, one can sympathise with Wolf's impatience and feel that some of the ideas were either insufficiently individual in their raw shape or else had cooled off into some less characteristic shape whilst being recollected in too much tranquillity.

A curious feature is the large amount of space, in the context, allotted to the second subject and its aftermaths, so that out of an exposition of 160 bars 111 are, with only tiny deviations, in D minor or D major. This renders rather comical the succession of cadence figures towards the double bar which painstakingly reinforce an already obvious key (see the exposition of the first movement of the C major Trio for an obvious contrast). The recapitulation redresses some of this imbalance by using some of the material for a transition, leaving the remainder wholly in G minor. The tendency to end a minor-key movement still in the minor seems to be a natural penchant of Brahms's mind, just as the reverse was the norm with Haydn. The Piano Quartet in C minor admits a late gleam of major into its finale, only to thrust it aside. The Third Symphony in F, although not a parallel case since it allows itself to end with a similar major-key sunset to that of its first movement, shows the same temperament by embarking in the last movement into an F minor storm for which no warning signals were hoisted at all.

The character piece which follows was originally called Scherzo. Its 9/8 time combines two triplet pulses, the ♪♪♪ usually in repeated notes being at fast scherzo speed whereas the ♩. beat is minuet-like. The unusual phrase-lengths and subtle scoring with muted strings lend it a great charm wholly individual to Brahms, although its fleeting dexterities sometimes seem to be echoed by Fauré, and one of the themes is reminiscent of Mendelssohn's *Ruy Blas* overture. Although here the 'symphonic' problems are in abeyance, a close analysis of the order of events will offer subtle surprises. For instance the *Ruy Blas* theme, which is the first thing the piano plays, is initially treated as a mere pendant to the main subject, and the second time it is heard (on the strings) it is used as a transition, by subtle extension, to the 'second subject'. It then disappears, as though it had fulfilled its minor structural task, only to reappear towards the end of the scherzo proper, not as a pendant to, but almost as a substitute for, the main subject, whimsically oscillating between major and minor.

The slow movement's basic design is a broad theme nobly sustained, flanking a dotted-rhythm fanfare-cum-march (albeit still in three time) which is given first *pp* and then *ff*. There is a big and deliberate disparity between these materials, and the transitions are beautifully done, especially the beginning of the reprise of the main theme in the secondary key and its flowering as it regains its home key.

The last movement doubtless had Haydn's famous Gypsy Rondo from his Piano Trio, Op. 1, as its exemplar. Its rhythm is perhaps its most striking feature – we go 78 bars before we escape from 3-bar phrases. Its design is, for Brahms, strikingly sectional, and it is only in the course of what amounts to a written-out cadenza that these particular barriers fall in a headlong rush home to the *molto presto*, a tempo marking unique in the chamber music.

Allegro non troppo: Poco adagio: Scherzo (Poco allegro): Finale (Allegro).

Brahms's essays in new media (e.g. symphonies, string quartets, sextets) often come in pairs, as though the way had been cleared for the second by the rigours of the first creative act. The sunny D major Second Symphony takes its ease in the citadel stormed by its C minor predecessor. This sunny and appealing second piano quartet, which figured in the public concert by which Brahms introduced himself to Vienna in 1862, is a similar complement to the gravity of the first. It is full of the happiness of a young man who had found himself, had found his way, and had been found, thanks to Schumann, Joachim and others, by the professional world of Germany and Austria. Significantly, the dedication is to Frau Dr Elisabeth Rösing who gave him, whilst he composed, the quiet and spaciousness of her house in the then sylvan retreat of Hamm – facilities not obtainable in the family home in Hamburg, dearly as he loved it.

The first movement is so lyrical that there are very few bars without hummable melodic content. Even the energetic moments are song-like. The linked procession of the exposition, whereby a foreground feature of one theme evolves from an unobtrusive background feature of a former one, is a beautiful example of the art of transition, though indeed 'transition', with its implication of a period spent getting from somewhere to somewhere else, seems a misnomer. It is of course calculated, as almost all composition is.

The sequence of keys is as orthodox as the structure, except for one surprise: the climactic statement of one of the themes in A minor, a key which one hardly expects immediately before a recapitulation beginning in A. Indeed one might have thought of the recapitulation, with its themes differently ordered, as beginning at that climax, if the position of Brahms's double bar did not contradict the idea. In fact, as often happens when the exposition is so carefully and richly woven, the order of events is undisturbed in the recapitulation, and the coda is a lingering farewell.

The rapt, nocturne-like slow movement, beginning and ending with the strings muted, points the paradox and charm of Brahms. It is one of his most individual and haunting pieces, and yet any descriptive analysis will make it sound like a pastiche of his predecessors' ideas. Take the first five bars, for example:

Ex. 9

We can see in the 'shadowing' of the piano's song by the violin a reference to Schumann's similar shadowings in his Lieder accompaniments. In the violin part of the fifth bar we see a Schubertian 'echo' of the tune's previous bar – an echo which is not literal but which serves to give a breather to the right hand's 'voice', to return the harmony from dominant to tonic, and to fill out and confirm the *five-bar* first phrase. Pure Brahms is the luxurious thickening of the accompaniment by the thirds and sixths of the viola and cello, and the threes-against-twos in the second bar. Yet what an unsatisfactory phrase 'pure Brahms' is, when all five bars are pure Brahms – when indeed to some ears the movement is the spring rapture which parallels the autumnal slow movement of the Clarinet Quintet. Another irresistible reminder of Schubert is the sinking back of the second passionate minor-key section into the final varied reprise of the main theme.

The two keys, F minor and E major, are identical with those of the 'source', the equally rapt slow movement of Schubert's String Quintet in C. This reprise is not the only example in the movement of elaborate variation, again involving a Brahmsian tension – a luxuriant flowering controlled by a rigid adherence to the original phrase-lengths. There is an interesting 'reminiscence' in the middle of the movement just before the reprise (bars 75–7): the music is momentarily Beethoven, in key (B major), in harmony and in melodic outline – see the slow movement of the *Emperor* – and the homage is that of Brahms the concert-pianist.

Although the third movement is still called Scherzo it is by and large of a type to which Brahms would later have denied the name. The graceful sinuosity of the opening tune puts an amiable rather than demonic gloss on the word, which even the stormier minor-key canonic writing of the Trio does not wholly disturb, although its far from easy octaves have something of the D minor Piano Concerto about them. Another unusual feature of this Trio is that the rhythm of its subsidiary *dolce* theme (bars 233–41) is identical with that of the scherzo's main theme – a device as sophisticated as it is unobtrusive. A possible criticism of the movement is that its transitions, ingenious though they are, seem sometimes disproportionate to what follows them, but this may be part of the general relaxation.

The finale does not aim so much at capping the other movements as complementing them, which it does by using a main theme of strongly marked rhythms and a plethora of contrasting other themes to make a mood which Beethoven might have recognised as 'unbuttoned'. Not that Brahms does not button up the music from time to time with intellectual *jeux d'esprit* such as contractions of rhythms from their normal lengths to shorter ones which induce a seeming acceleration, with the bar-lines momentarily forgotten.

Ex. 10

(Violin, + Cello an octave lower)

(Piano)

This technique is found again in, for example, the last movement of the violin concerto and indeed in the closing *allegro* of Brahms's last chamber work, the Clarinet Sonata, Op. 120, no. 2. It is perhaps merely a reflection of our less leisured tastes that the recapitulation of the procession of secondary themes seems rather long, especially as it involves hearing four times a modulation (to and from a key a major third lower) which is to our ears a blatant imitation of Schubert. The final *animato* peroration possibly exceeds the true functions of the four players, who in trying to emulate a symphony risk sounding like a teashop.

PIANO QUARTET NO. 3 IN C MINOR, OP. 60

Allegro non troppo: Scherzo (Allegro): Andante: Finale (Allegro comodo).

Although this work was not published till 1875 Brahms conceived its first movement (in C sharp minor until Joachim dissuaded him) and slow movement as early as 1855, in the period of emotional turmoil at Düsseldorf when he stayed with Clara Schumann during the dreadful days of Schumann's last illness. Brahms revealed his state of mind in a letter to Hermann Deiters: 'Just picture to yourself a man who is going to shoot himself . . .', and again to Theodor Billrot: 'This quartet is only communicated as a curiosity, say as an illustration to the last chapter of the Man with the Blue Jacket and Yellow Vest.' The allusion is to Goethe's 'hero' Werther, whose sorrows and suicide epitomised the Sturm und Drang movement which heralded literary romanticism as early as 1774.

After a loud unison on the piano, the strings propound the first subject, which is not so much a theme as a downward progression beginning with the rhythm 3/4 ♩ ♩ 𝄽 which, *legato* or *staccato*, permeates much of the movement. The answering phrase elongates itself into a striking series of chromatically groping, downward chords. But this is almost the last significant material in the movement for the strings, the texture being soon dominated, sometimes fiercely so, by the piano. The movement was sketched alongside parts of the first piano concerto, and the strings are too often used in rather ungainly accompaniment figures or in vehement doubling which seems to reach out for more sonority than the medium can give. After a short storm and a lengthy *diminuendo* the second subject (and here it is right to use the singular) is announced on the piano. By a most unusual procedure it occupies almost all the rest of the exposition, although a first glance at the score might not show it. It is an eight-bar phrase to which are immediately added three free variations and a climactic restatement. Phrase-lengths are varied as well as tune, but the whole achieves a remarkable continuity until the ♩ ♩ 𝄾 rhythm marks the end of the exposition. After the previous orthodox keys the development storms far afield and comes to an end as the whole 'orchestra' takes up the triplet rhythm of the 'drums' which the bass of the piano has been playing for twenty bars. There is some major-key tranquillity as the variations, further diversified and lengthened, recur in the recapitulation, but there is never any real prospect of any other than a minor-key ending to a movement which is much more powerful than lovable.

From the first movement's C minor fierceness we go to the C minor fierceness of the scherzo, written somewhat later. Though there is inevitably some piano-pounding and some clouds of rosin it is part and parcel of the effect of vehement struggle, and Brahms has achieved an altogether more equitable distribution of instrumental interest. There are two themes which afford momentary relief from the prevailing galloping tensions: the first is not so much a theme as an epigrammatic series of chords announced first on the strings alone; the second, also first heard on the strings, is more lyrical and *legato* and might have been called 'Trio' did it not plunge without a break into a prolonged and exciting transition to the recapitulation – a passage which presages the rhythmic ardours of the last movement of the D minor Violin Sonata.

At last the *andante* brings the major key (of E) and comparative repose, with the strings allowed to sing to the piano's accompaniment. The elaboration of some of the texture is counterbalanced by the simple, unhurried sonata-form design.

The finale is chiefly notable for the nearly perpetual motion of its pattering accompaniment. Brahms is not ostensibly taking up the cudgels again but instead allows the violin a long solo to introduce the plaintive theme, whose principal feature is the falling third with which it opens. The other notable subject consists of five-bar chorale-like phrases for the strings which are almost the only occasions when the accompaniment stops. Towards the end these recur in C major, but the last pages, though marked *tranquillo*, still have a heavy admixture of the minor. The man with the blue jacket and yellow vest has the last word.

Strings alone - Sextets, Quintets, Quartets

SEXTET NO. I IN B FLAT, OP. 18

Allegro ma non troppo: Andante, ma moderato: Scherzo (Allegro molto): Rondo (Poco allegro e grazioso).

The unusual medium is exploited immediately, for although only three instruments are playing we have a first-cello tune with a second-cello bass and a viola between them, producing a sonority unobtainable from a string quartet. The immediate restatement also avoids the quartet, being for five, and before thirty bars are up we even have one of the six instruments double-stopping. Though the tune is broad in its effect we have the characteristic avoidance, by sophisticated doublings back on itself, of 4- and 8-bar phrases. In bar 31 the gapped arpeggio throwing emphasis on the sixth makes an early appearance and is the main feature of the main secondary subject (Ex. 11(i)). It is a Brahms fingerprint (e.g. the last bar of Ex. 1, and many places in the Third Symphony). Amongst the manipulations should be noted the ancient device of diminution applied to the opening of the main theme (Ex. 11(ii) becoming (iii)) and the transformation of its final phrase (note again the falling sixth – Ex. 11(iv)) into the beginning of a 'new' tune in the far-away key of A (Ex. 11(v)).

Ex. 11

The three rising crotchets marked with a bracket are yet another fingerprint, used sometimes to form an 'up-beat' bar, sometimes as the accented bar, often, as in this movement, using both positions in the same musical paragraph. The first movement incidentally prefigures the well-known chorus from the *Requiem* – 'How lovely are Thy dwellings' – in its triple-time suavity of melody and sometimes (bars 76–9) in harmony as well.

The sonata-form outlines of the movement are entirely ortho-dox, with the second subject group in the dominant. Clearly Brahms's instinct for poise and measure told him that the infinite possibilities of variation afforded by the unusual texture made a wide enough field for himself and his audience to explore. (It was probably for the same reason that he chose variation form for the slow movement.) There is even, as far as structure goes, a con-siderable identity between exposition and recapitulation. The first subject begins as at Ex. 11(ii) but an octave lower on the first cello; towards its close, now on the sextet's full euphony, it incorporates Ex. 11(i) and (iv). Ex. 11(iii) helps it to wind through a transition, which hesitates momentarily before stepping into the far distance with Ex. 11(v), whose notes by a typical touch of scoring are doubled an octave lower, although this involves low-lying major thirds (C♯ in A). The second subject (again announced by the first cello) has obviously germinated from Ex. 11(i), and its pendant takes up its quaver rhythm (Ex. 11(vi)).

The exposition closes with *pizzicato* accompaniments of what sounds like Beethoven no. 7 turned into a Viennese waltz. Such vigour as the development allows itself derives from Ex. 11(vi), which now takes on an air of *Egmont*. The *pizzicato* waltz, in slower tempo, momentarily spreads to all the players at the end.

The second movement varies a D minor theme which soars but is rendered four-square by the insistent spondees below. Again, typically, it is first stated by the four lower instruments making five-part harmony, thanks to double stops, and again there is hardly a bar which could be played by a string quartet. Until the music turns to the major key the variations use the traditional device (e.g. Handel's *Harmonious Blacksmith*, Beethoven's Arietta from his last piano sonata) of introducing in successive variations quicker subdivisions of the beat. There is a nice bagpipe effect for two violas in the fifth variation, and indeed Brahms's com-parative conservatism in orchestral colour is conspicuously absent from the chamber music, especially these earlier works which break away from the quartet archetype.

The *allegro molto* of the scherzo is an unequivocal marking which became rarer. It is a succinct and vigorous piece with, for once, a non-relaxing trio. One is reminded of the trio of the scherzo of Beethoven's Fifth Symphony (as of his *Egmont* overture in the first movement) by the prominent ♫♫ | ♩ figure.

Of the Rondo Joachim wrote to Brahms: 'I expected a little more force at the end and wish the second subject had more contrast to the first.' There is some justice in this impression, and the occasional bursts of energy can seem rather factitious, but such fallings-off, if they be so, have a tradition of relaxation behind them, Schubert being the obvious example.

SEXTET NO. 2 IN G, OP. 36

Allegro non troppo: Scherzo (Allegro non troppo): Adagio: Poco allegro.

Alternating semitones, first heard on the first viola, ripple through much of the first movement, which is also dominated by the rising fifths of the main subject,

Ex. 12

which of course fall when inverted and then have the effect of assenting phrases at the end of the sentences. The development section demonstrates the inversions on a larger scale, and the effortless counterpoint slowly unfolding gives the work a cooler feel than the warm-bath harmony of the preceding sextet, although the six instruments continue to be fully employed. The development also begins to use the semitone alternations in a different way which is simple but striking. Whereas in the exposition the accented note (the first of each pair) is part of the harmony, now it is sometimes the second of the pair which fits the harmony, making of the first an incidental ornament. A captivating example of the sudden change of harmony involved is this glide from A major to C♯ minor:

Note especially how in the last bar of the example the As are now dissonant with the G sharp of the tune emerging below. This is but one of the constant instances in Brahms of technical ingenuities used to poetic effect, where the mere description of the process makes Brahms sound like a knitter, not a poet. The genial and relaxed feel of this movement is partly due to the unusual number, for Brahms, of balancing phrases and to the recapitulation of long stretches of music which are rescored but not reconstructed. Presumably for the same reason as in the previous sextet the sonata form is quite orthodox, but as to incidental detail the choice for mention is endless and arbitrary. However, in any count Agathe von Siebold must have her due, as being the one young lady to whom Brahms was ever engaged. She was the pretty-voiced, pretty-figured daughter of a Göttingen professor, and the musical letters of her name are enshrined in a motif first heard towards the end of the exposition:

The end of the development draws itself together by a more insistent confrontation of the second half of Ex. 12 with its inversion, until a climax is made with both versions simultaneously at top and bottom with the rippling quavers now foaming between. The beginning of the coda, after Agathe has had her last say, is marked by a slightly slower tempo and a beautiful modulation in the first subject reserved for this moment.

In the scherzo the duple time, the tonic minor key and above all the *non troppo* tell their own tale. We might expect that, despite the title, Brahms in these grave measures was setting out to write an Anti-scherzo, had not a *presto giocoso* by way of middle section broken out in the major with a galumphing bass like a Ländler exceeding the speed limit.

In the *adagio* a wayward melody in the minor is clothed in gaunt chromatic harmonies and then presented in variations whose tenuous melodic connection with the theme is compensated by the rigidity with which the phrase-lengths and the cadential modulations are reproduced (a trait, incidentally, which is particularly evident in the Paganini variations for piano). This is another example of Brahms's 'new wine in old bottles' technique. The final variation (*adagio*, major) includes a device common in Brahms's calm 'all-passion-spent' mood: the use of pairs of instruments, in this case mainly the violas, to play imitation horn-calls up and down whilst the harmony stands still for the purpose.

Even in the finale we still have an easy-going *poco allegro* marking. In spite of the busy fugued writing in the development and, *animato*, in the coda, the movement is decidedly of the relaxing type, with little unexpected structure. The main *legato* theme (in the fifth bar) marked *tranquillo* and later *semplice* begins with the rising scale which occurs so often in triple time (see the first sextet), and here indeed the 9/8 key signature, by subdividing the three main beats into three, gives us the ultimate in 'triplicity' and a correspondingly suave and relaxed utterance. The 9/4 second subject of the Third Symphony evokes the same feeling.

STRING QUINTET NO. I IN F, OP. 88

Allegro non troppo ma con brio: Grave ed appassionato, alternating with *Allegretto vivace* and *Presto: Allegro energico*.

Elisabeth von Herzogenberg paid the first movement an odd compliment: 'It is refreshing to see the framework exposed in such bald, prosaic fashion.' The *non troppo* and the *poco forte* invite the players to hold their horses before they are out of the stable. After the deployment of a not very bold tune the liveliness of the subsequent dotted rhythms seems somewhat factitious. The second subject is in A, a bright, 'sharpening' effect because the new key involves the raising of both the principal notes – tonic and dominant – of the old. This relationship was to be explored again in the almost contemporary Third Symphony. In this quintet the modulation is made by a dominant seventh followed by a silence (one of Elisabeth's 'bald, prosaic' features?).

Its swinging triplets on the first viola are overlaid with contra-dictory rhythms – 3 against 4, 3 against 2 – which tend to cloud what freshness the original impulse may have had. The feeling of going through impressive motions persists in the development, and apart from a few moments of genuine passion, manipulation, albeit such as few of Brahms's contemporaries could achieve, remains the order of the day. But it is worth noting the long pedal-point in the development, a device taken over so as to encompass the whole development section in the first movement of the D minor Violin Sonata.

On the other hand the second movement is one of Brahms's most imaginative constructions. It is a sandwich of slower and faster tempi such as are also found in the Second Symphony and Second Violin Sonata. The opening *grave* is taken from a sarabande for piano which he wrote as an exercise in Baroque-style pastiche in 1855. The scoring is unusual and resourceful (for instance the opening bars have the tune in thirds but with the cello above the first violin) and the music is the more poignant in that it begins in the major key and it is only in the fifth bar that it is suffused with the minor. This section gives way to a graceful *allegretto* whose dotted rhythms have a touch of the Liebeslieder waltzes about them, and this in turn disappears into silence after ambiguous harmony. The question as to which key the harmony portends is resolved by a yet more elaborate and impassioned version of the opening sarabande. This further swing of the pendulum is balanced by a feather-light transformation of the *allegretto* into a *presto*, but its first paragraph, with Brahmsian integrity, follows precisely the phrase-lengths of its original – it is as though Brahms sets out on these flights of fancy with a para-chute which is sure to open. The final statement of the sarabande takes up the key of the faster music (A), then works back to its own original C sharp major/minor, including a beautiful passage originating in an inversion of the main subject. This inversion can in turn be traced back to the place in the original 'exercise' sarabande where a man of Brahms's erudition following Bach's footsteps could not fail to consider an inversion. The music sub-sides to long and soft alternations of the two basic keys, and as a crowning surprise ends in the A major which, not being the 'home' of the movement, is the less expected of the two.

The final movement, with its near-perpetual-motion fugal

style, is reminiscent of Smetana's *Bartered Bride* overture, which had conquered Europe since it was first heard in 1866. Unlike Brahms's earlier example of a fugal opening (in the last movement of the first Cello Sonata) the music is here of an ebullient jollity. The two punctuating chordal hammer-strokes make a fine climactic surprise when the rhythm is dislocated by the elongation of the silence between them (bars 20–1), a particularly powerful effect since it is on the first beat of the bar that the unexpected silence falls. For the secondary materials the music again moves from F to A. This duplication of the first movement's tonal centres (F, A, F) might be a reference to Brahms's personal motto 'Frei aber froh' (free but happy): certainly, taken in conjunction with the central movement's complementary use of A arrived at from the opposite direction ($C\sharp \rightarrow A$) it argues a carefully balanced piece of long-range tonal engineering. Typical of Brahms is his passing of a variant of the fugato subject through the upper instruments with the marking *dolce semplice*, although the new curves of the variation are neither sweet nor simple on the face of it. After a momentary slowing of the persistent quavers to triplet crotchets Brahms ends with a real kicking-over-the-traces *presto*.

STRING QUINTET NO. 2 IN G, OP. 111

Allegro non troppo ma con brio: Adagio: Un poco allegretto: Vivace ma non troppo presto.

The sole cello delivering the ardently leaping first subject finds himself over-weighted by the pairs of violins and violas above, a curious miscalculation by one who had by then written far more chamber music than anyone of his generation.[1] Fervour and ebullience are such a feature of this movement that to restrain the top for the sake of the bottom seems contrary to the natural impulsiveness of the music. All the secondary themes are luxuriously scored, the first beginning with a viola duet and sometimes employing a typical and charming subdivision of the nine quavers in a bar thus: 1 2 3 4 5 6 7 8 9. The second is first heard on the

[1] Geiringer, in *Brahms: His life and work* (London, 1936) quotes on p. 242 Brahms's autograph thinning of the violin and viola parts here. But Brahms allowed the original to stand in print.

second violin and is characterised by a rising third. The rising third softly and slowly rises from the beginning of the development, whose onset is marked by a sudden change of key and by the first *pianissimo* of the movement. The great variety of the development is all the more remarkable when one considers that out of its 49 bars there is only one (the first) in which any instrument has a whole bar's rest, and in 31 bars there are double stops (at least) making a total of six or more simultaneous notes from the five instruments. Indeed in one bar, marked *pesante* to boot, there are actually six *nine*-part chords in succession. The blood was still red in 1891.

The slow movement is a minor-key march, perhaps referring back in spirit to the slow movement of the sextet, Op. 18; but whereas the former was a straightforward set of variations, this movement although mainly lyrical and fairly brief – 80 bars – is one of Brahms's subtlest creations. Structurally it entirely lacks the measured modulation and the ensuing new paragraph implied by the term 'second subject', yet it is not monolithic. Its variety lies in the ever-shifting implied keys of the main (and indeed the only) subject, which itself contains the sort of disparate phrases from which only a master could feel confident of making ultimate coherence. For instance, the first two bars (violas over *pizzicato* cello) could be in D minor or A major; without any transition the third bar launches into a C major chord which, however, seems the next moment to be in A minor. These creative ambiguities continue until the first viola soaring high and cadenza-like brings the music home, having traversed a great range of feeling and variety of texture.

After this the third movement serves as a relaxed intermezzo, not demonstrative except of constructional skill. There is a wistful main theme in the minor, unusually regular in the balance of its phrases. The contrasting major-key section has short, graceful alternating duets for violas and violins. The easy-going feeling is heightened by a literal repetition of the whole minor section. The brief reminiscence of the major section begins with a near-inversion of its erstwhile opening phrase – perhaps a teasing allusion to unexpended reserves of creative energy.

In the finale a subject which begins away from its home key allows of Haydn-like witticisms. At the beginning we have nine bars *piano* led by the viola in what turns out to be the 'wrong'

key, with the violins reserved for the *forte* swing to the right key.
At the recapitulation the 'wrong' key evokes a furious *fortissimo*,
on the heels of which the 'right' key glides in quietly and sweetly,
with an immediate *pizzicato* repeat to cap the effect almost before
the ear has time to accept its gratification. Just before the end a
rush of unison semiquavers makes to end in a suspiciously square
and trite cadence; sure enough, this cadence is interrupted, and
the interruption is permanent because the overdone cadence was
in the 'wrong' key. At this point the music adopts the 'Gipsy-
Hungarian' style in strong reminiscence of the First Piano Quartet,
but whereas that used three-bar phrases most of these are of five
bars. The piece is notable for a real sense of *allegro* movement, the
development in particular achieving a great sense of energy by
compressing wide-ranging harmonies into a short time-span. Ad-
mirable too in the thematic transitions is the certainty of judge-
ment which decides how 'tuneful' such passages should be – in
other words how to write melodic motifs that will not be mistaken
for 'subjects', and with harmonies that will feel transitional.
Many apprentice composers who have struggled with these things
cannot but envy the expertise even if the idiom is unfashionable.

STRING QUARTET, OP. 51, NO. 1 IN C MINOR

Allegro: Romanze (Poco adagio): Allegretto molto moderato e comodo:
Allegro.

Brahms himself declared that he had written many string quartets
before this, but as with the symphony this first *published* excursion
into a 'classical' medium *par excellence* comes comparatively late.
Curiously enough, C minor is the key with which Brahms broke
the ice in the symphony. Is there perhaps some clue to Brahms's
character here – the act of girding the loins causing him to grit the
teeth as well? Grittiness is certainly in evidence in this quartet,
and in its first movement a high proportion of what can most
kindly be called non-melodic work. The viola is a particular
sufferer, with a great deal of harmonic filling-up in remorseless
quavers, and exposed moments (bars 7–8, 143–4) when after
detached chords from his colleagues he sustains, *fp*, an octave
and demonstrates how inferior he is to the couple of horns which
Brahms should have been using for the job. 'Orchestral' writing

for single strings can be too easily and unimaginatively criticised. Much depends on the quality of the music, and a sense of strain may in itself play a part in the music's effect, particularly indeed in Brahms. Experienced listeners will have favourite 'orchestral' passages in chamber music. (One which leaves an indelible impression comes in the slow movement of Schubert's G major Quartet, where in vivid and almost inconsequential alternation there are unison ejaculations and stormy, thick tremolandi – the very stuff which one would think the orchestra could do much better, yet thrilling in their sense of struggle which contrasts so finely with the touching, wistful music of the rest of the movement.) But in this Brahms movement there is a shortage of telling melody combined with a good deal of sheer ungainliness. The harmonic richness which can so often counterbalance it has a factitious feel to it, and too long a slice of the recapitulation consists of traversing exactly the same ground with no alteration except transposition, a process which needs a greater richness of material to justify a second hearing. Nevertheless it is difficult to suppose that an experienced composer, having waited so long to publish, would have spent the time and trouble merely to make a petulant gesture so likely to antagonise a public – a public which we must remember would buy quartets in order to play them at home. There is a tongue-tied rhetoric here. Such drama as it has lies precisely in the feeling of fighting against odds, against an intractable medium, against the knowledge perhaps that on this occasion there would be no winning through to the haven where we would be – that if there were to be sweetness and light others had already expressed it ineffably in the same medium. On this view we can feel involved in a drama in which the constantly recurring first subject (Ex. 15) constantly summons a storm, as it were, to drown any incipient songs.

Ex. 15
Allegro

When it is not a storm, it is a cloud – witness the subject's effect when played on the cello at the end of both exposition and recapitulation, where it twice extinguishes a momentary glimpse of the major key.

Brahms gives little away by his movement titles. What the term 'Romanze' meant to him in 1873 is difficult to guess. For Mozart (e.g. in the Piano Concerto in D minor, K.466) or for Beethoven in the two Romances for violin it might have implied a folk-song-like simplicity of theme and form. Here we have the simple form – an alternation of slightly related paragraphs A,B,A,B, virtually without transitions and without large-scale modulation – but the melodies are sophisticated in their phrase-lengths and incidental modulations, and the second 'A' of the scheme is a variation of the first, in which a rigorous reproduction of the harmonies offsets a very free melodic elaboration. Perhaps the 'romance' is found in the persistent evocation of softly rising horn-calls in the main theme, and in the sighing effect of the triplet chords, often lacking the first of the three, of the secondary material.

The next movement can only be regarded as even a substitute scherzo by using the adjective 'whimsical' rather than 'plaintive'. The whimsicality lies in the contrast between the persistent drooping contours and low dynamic level of the subject-matter and the obscured tonality of much of the piece – an intended contrast which can be deduced from Brahms's mark of *semplice* over a passage which in these respects is *not* simple. The 'Trio' is a marked contrast: the duple time gives way to a faster triple time and what is by comparison an obvious melody accompanied for most of its length by an alternation of an open-string and stopped-string A on the second violin.

These two short but leisurely movements leave the way clear for a real *allegro* by way of finale. The dotted rhythm of the opening unison gesture is never far away, and in such a place as bars 12–14 comes close to being an outright reference to the main subject of the first movement. The following example shows the 'gesture' in brackets; the whole example shows bars 12–14 for comparison with Ex. 15.

Ex. 16

The intended energy is not wholly convincing as the melodies lack character, and there are also passages of close imitation whose effect depends on a quick articulation, low on the cello, of figuration which is unlikely to be achieved. But the form is interesting in the ambiguous use of the opening gesture after the exposition. Does it mark the beginning of a development, or is there no development proper in the sense of a defined working-out section, only a recapitulation containing some development after the opening gesture? The ambiguity is of course planned, as is the unambiguous drawing of the threads together by a prolonged reference, in a stormy coda, to the first subject, which decisively insists on the minor key when the signs were that we were to relax into the major. Here again a bigger sonority seems to be called for than the four players can provide. Dr Theodor Billrot, the dedicatee of both the Op. 51 quartets - a friend of Brahms as intimate as any – must have felt he was invited to put that in his pipe and smoke it.

STRING QUARTET, OP. 51, NO. 2 IN A MINOR

Allegro non troppo: Andante moderato: Quasi menuetto (moderato)
alternating with *Allegretto vivace: Finale (Allegro non assai).*

This companion quartet is also in the minor key, and indeed its four movements all have the same keynote. The first movement acutely poses a problem which is never far from the surface with Brahms, and one which arises, ironically enough, from the honesty of his thought and the integrity of his workmanship. It may not arise with a composer intent on covering his tracks, or with one who blunders less skilfully down partly new tracks. But the fact remains that the first movement reads and sounds like a determined demonstration of the mechanics of sonata form, as though Brahms had conscientiously addressed himself to the question put by the Lord to Ezekiel in the valley of the vision: 'Can these bones live?' It is all impeccably done, after the very best models. But coming at least a generation after its models its form cannot be regarded as simply arising from the material in a first fine careless rapture; the material is too palpably manipulated for that. The expected keys are reached by the expected transitions at the expected time. Even Brahms's marvellous arts of variation are in abeyance – except for an ornamented first-subject reprise – with 66 consecutive bars, almost half the exposition, reappearing virtually unaltered in the recapitulation, except for transposition.

Even the technical writing is not happy: the viola's share in the second subject hardly compensates him for the awkward triplet accompaniments which frequently fall to him. The triplets usually conflict with duplets elsewhere, and in lyrical passages one longs for the piano's sustaining pedal, which in these circumstances makes all the difference between warmth and restlessness. When the movement stirs itself to an accelerating coda the effect is much weakened (bars 315 ff.) by a threefold conflict of rhythms.

The main subject of the second movement, at first presented with an angular counterpoint in octaves for viola and cello, is involuted and rhythmically sophisticated, but the subsidiary material, a close and spectacular violin/cello canon with trembling accompaniment, and a coda theme which achieves true sweetness with a melody which later served Richard Strauss in *Don Juan*, raise the music to new heights of interest, as does the recapitulation in a 'wrong' key whose righting by the cello is a highlight of the movement. The foreign key is F in the context of A – yet another example of the F/A relationship which was always lurking in Brahms's mind. It is interesting to see how the emotional plan is served by the progressive smoothing-out of the angular two-part counterpoint of the opening: at the F major recapitulation it is transferred to the second violin and viola whilst the cello sustains an F below to anchor it and tame it, as it were; then in the A major recapitulation, where the cello plays the tune, it is absorbed into rich harmony, whilst at the end all that remain are its opening three notes, which are concordant in any case.

The third movement is another ingenious scherzo-substitute. It begins in the same key and in the same wistful, rather than playful, manner as the corresponding movement in the First Cello Sonata, but here we are teased by a constant succession of three-bar phrases. For 'Trio' we have a change of speed and mode (major for minor). Its affinities with the minuetto emerge toward the end of each of its two balancing sections, and are underlined in the snatch of the original tempo which occurs half-way.

In spite of the cautionary *non assai* of the last movement a good deal of the extravert brio of a scherzo rubs off on it. Some of the actual matter of the preceding movement rubs off too. The two opening subjects, for example, are markedly similar in their melodic shapes and their three-bar phrases. Telling inspirations are the alteration of the three-bar phrase to a four-bar one in mid-movement and its tightening to two bars in the coda, which throws off the enticements of languor and at last offers drastic energy of expression.

STRING QUARTET NO. 3 IN B FLAT, OP. 67

Vivace: Andante: Agitato (Presto non troppo): Poco allegretto con variazioni.

After the stern and rather stiff gestures of the Op. 51 pair we find in Op. 67, if not the break-through to an assured matching of music and quartet-technique, at least a good-humoured un-buttoning of ideas. This relaxation is evident in the first movement which mingles 6/8 horn-calls (by association with Mozart's *Hunt* Quartet in the same key?) and the 2/4 rhythms of Czech dances. There are teasing Beethovenish key-changes connected by silences rather than transitions. The 2/4 and 6/8 rhythms not only alternate but coincide, and there are paragraphs of relaxed happiness where one could almost call Brahms garrulous, of all epithets!

The theme of the slow movement, after two introductory bars, is couched in three successive balancing eight-bar phrases, in itself a rarity in Brahms. This symmetry is offset by a central section which modulates restlessly and widely and which even uses two 5/4 bars. Serenity is regained in a fine example of a varied reprise, beginning in a foreign key and gradually losing its elaboration as it settles into the home tonic.

The third movement is a technical *tour de force* of composition. If the average listener doesn't hear it as such, that is a measure of the technique's success. It is a movement in which the viola takes the lead. There are obvious acoustical problems in getting the middle of a texture into prominence, and one means, adopted here, is to mute the other instruments. But this in turn means that whatever its momentary role the viola will sound differently from, and indeed louder than, the others for every single bar. This is not such a problem if the other instruments are to be nonentities throughout, but a movement so constructed would be a boring denial of the individual dialogue implicit in the classical ideal of the string quartet.

Brahms makes room for the first theme by allowing nothing

else on the first beats of the bar (this makes an effect like an assenting sigh from the viola's companions) and by ensuring that on the last beats of the bar the viola is frequently the top voice:

Ex. 17

When this phrase is shortly repeated it is given to the violin (still not occupying the first beat), but since the viola cannot retreat to anonymity it has a running variation not unlike that found in Baroque chorale preludes (the 'melody notes' in the viola part are marked with x):

Ex. 18

(Harmony on 2nd Violin and *pizzicato* Cello)

Another means of distributing melodic interest is to write pairs of themes in counterpoint. Ex. 19 illustrates the 'twinning' of first violin and viola, who alternate their material four bars at a time. Note that at the third bar the melody which the viola has started goes off the bottom of its range and has to be taken by the cello (see the arrow); but the viola cannot disappear, and instead makes a virtue of its different timbre and uses it to punctuate and sustain the harmony as a pair of horns would.

Brahms has not called this movement Scherzo or Minuet (a salon-music composer might have called it 'Wistful Waltz') but nevertheless calls its middle section Trio. Perhaps this whimsicality was suggested by a further solution of the viola problem; he starts off with a real trio, excluding the viola. It is strongly characterised: by the all-muted sound, heard here for the first

Ex. 19

time, by the melodic shape, considerably enhanced by the cello going mainly in the opposite direction, by the captivating waltz-rhythm with alternate first beats still empty, and by the dynamics twice making frustrated crescendos before finding their climax. It all amounts to a 'subject' experienced in its own right, and yet in a few moments the whole thing turns, unaltered, into a background for the viola's tune. (The reader will have first to imagine the example without its viola part):

Ex. 20

We have frequently noticed the basic strictness of Brahms's variations, anchoring and deepening his fancy. In this finale the

quirks of modulation and rhythm are built into the theme (Ex. 21).
Note how the first half uses four symmetrical bars and swerves
aside to D instead of the usual dominant (F). In the complementary second half Brahms remains in D for four bars, leading
us to suppose that with the return to B flat another four bars will
round it off. Instead we have to make do with the comic abrupt-
ness of only two. Note also the sophisticated variations and uses
of the phrase in brackets:

Ex. 21

In the first two variations the viola seems unwilling to surrender
the leadership. We turn to the minor for the fourth variation and
further afield for the fifth and sixth. With the seventh we return
not only to the original key but unmistakably to the figuration
of the first movement's main subject, whilst still clothing the
basic shape of the variations. This effect is easier heard than seen,
but the following example gives the beginning of the process.
The second violin and the viola are reverting to the horn-like
subject of the work's opening. Two bars of this extract are the
equivalent of one bar of the variation theme (Ex. 21), and to
facilitate the comparison some notes are marked with *x*:

Ex. 22

Nor is this all, for another change to the minor brings a variation
using further first-movement material. Compare this passage
from bars 257ff. of the first movement (Ex. 23(i)), where it forms
an introduction to the 'Czech dance' second subject, with its
ion use (ii), now with the all-important up-beats added:

Ex. 23 (i)

We cannot tell which use came first to mind. Such are the beautiful mysteries of composition. Only after this minor variation does the music burst its mould, though even here we get glimpses of the variation theme. After the final swerve to D major the balancing B flat is at last allowed not two bars but eleven, an event for which the whole movement seems to have been a preparation, a cool coup of a giant at play.

Trios

The Piano Trio in B, Op. 8, was originally completed and published in 1854, the autograph score being signed by Brahms as 'Kreisler junior', a reference to the quirky Kapellmeister Kreisler, a creation of the romantic novelist E. T. A. Hoffmann. The same character lent his name to Schumann's suite of piano pieces, *Kreisleriana*, Op. 16; and indeed Kreisler and Hoffmann were twin idols of the Schumann circle to which young Brahms had been persuaded, mainly by his friend and colleague the violinist Joachim, to introduce himself the previous year. The music which Kreisler evoked both in Schumann and (given some differences in temperament) Brahms could be characterised as a mixture of frank, even ebullient, ardour with a sometimes whimsical tenderness, the music, like Kreisler, being given to unexpected turns of phrase and direction.

If some of these terms seem at variance with the Brahms we know it has to be remembered that the version of this work which is almost always played is the sweeping revision of 1891. It is a far cry from the impetuosity of the heart-(almost)-on-sleeve Brahms in his twenties to the eagle-eyed, exigent self-criticism objectively probing for weaknesses whose remedies ranged from minute alterations to pages of rewriting.[1] Thus we naturally, but unhistorically, tend to regard the virtually suppressed first version as uncharacteristic, and are inclined to forget that for eight years, until the appearance in 1862 of the Sextet in B flat, Op. 18, it held its own as the only, and highly esteemed, published chamber work of Brahms. In this context it is interesting to note the obvious imprint of the Schumann milieu on the piano pieces having the next two opus numbers. Op. 9 is a set of variations paying tribute to Schumann not only by using a theme of his but by evoking and perhaps surpassing his penchant for contrapuntal dexterity at the keyboard. Op. 10 is a set of Ballades; the first is prefaced by a quotation *in extenso* of the bloodthirsty Scottish ballad *Edward*, whose words the main theme fits (see also the 'folk-song' slow movement of the First Piano Sonata and also the opening, to quoted 'folk' words, of the well-known Intermezzo in E flat, Op. 117); the spirit of Schumann unmistakably hovers over the main theme of the fourth Ballade of Op. 10 (compare this dreaming, nostalgic waltz with the A major theme, for example, from the seventh of Schumann's *Novelletten* for piano, Op. 21).

It is a moot point whether we are ever justified in performing as 'Brahms' a version which was so clearly disowned by the composer. The same sort of consideration ought to forbid the performance of Mozart's Symphony No. 40 in G minor without clarinets when they are available, since Mozart lost no time in rescoring the piece – greatly to the clarinet's advantage *vis-à-vis* the oboe – as soon as the opportunity arose. With the hindsight of Brahms's reconstruction we can see ultimately unacceptable loosenesses of construction, chiefly centred in the character and deployment of the 'second-subject' paragraphs. But we may find the occasional performance of the first version of some interest, particularly in these very paragraphs, when we are in an historical

---

[1] For a perceptive and readable comparison see Hans Gal, *Johannes Brahms*, ed by Joseph Stein, pp. 155 ff.

frame of mind, or even when we merely find ourselves in the mood to value Kreislerish impulses above the ultimate integrities. As it will obviously be a convenience to listeners, each version is here described as a work in its own right, at the cost of some slight repetitions. After the two analyses there is a short comparative study.

PIANO TRIO NO. I IN B, OP 8 (FIRST VERSION, 1854)

Allegro con moto: Scherzo (Allegro molto): Adagio non troppo: Finale (Allegro molto agitato).

For what it is worth, the choice of B major for a work's basic key is virtually unprecedented, at least amongst the 'Viennese classics'. Mozart and Beethoven offer no examples, Haydn has one symphony (no. 46) and a lost string trio, Schubert a piano sonata.

The ardent main theme is heard first in the tenor register of the piano, to be shortly joined by another 'tenor', the cello, singing in thirds above, which with the frequent, rather Mendelssohnian, long appoggiaturas lends the whole opening a euphonious and expansive air. The theme has affinities, which some could feel amounted to pre-echoes, in the first movement of the Piano Sonata, Op. 1. Compare the opening of the trio (i), especially the harmonic-cum-melodic crunches marked x, with the version of the sonata's *Hammerklavier* opening (ii) and the more energetic version with a delayed top (iii):

Ex. 24 (i)

(ii)

(iii)

(Bass D _ _ _ _ D _ _ _ _ G# _ _ _ _)

The point is not the tiresome game of 'spot the resemblance', but the noting of a fingerprint of Brahms which remains for a lifetime, especially in the fervent diatonic tunes with which he often diversifies his scherzos – e.g., C major Trio, Op. 87, and for that matter the C major tune in the scherzo of Op. 1, which furnishes a particularly luxurious example in its fifth bar.

One can measure the expansiveness of the opening of this B major Trio by noting that in the twentieth bar, when the violin takes a hand in the main melodic work, we are still wedded to our home key and an only slight modification of the opening – as indeed is still the case at another restart at bar 35. It is eventually the first three falling notes of the main theme – first emphatically lengthened, then shortened and isolated – which cause the break-up of the suave paragraph and lead to a second paragraph. This begins in the relative minor key with a not wholly new tune (note the three falling notes) delivered in quiet octaves on the piano as though it might become a fugal subject:

Ex. 25

This turns out not to be the case, but it is taken up for a while by the strings in canon. This exploration in turn gives way to a horn-and-bagpipe pastoral tune, still related to the opening subject, in the orthodox dominant key of a second subject:

Ex. 26

It is the sort of 'momentary relaxation' material which is more succinctly used in the same place in the design in the first movement of the first Cello Sonata, Op. 38, but in this trio it does not come to rest but drifts back to the relative minor before the double-bar. The three falling notes, which have remained a ~~silent~~ ient ingredient, launch the development first almost imperceptibly, then tumble into a series of mainly energetic but somewhat sectional workings whose common derivation is shown to be the opening of the main theme. In a moment of quiet the 'pastoral' theme is again discussed, and its own derivation from the main theme becomes more apparent when it serves as the connecting thread in a long, rhythmically vigorous but harmonically rather static preparation for the recapitulation. Here is added a stretch of fugal work which was only threatened before, and a rather grandiose coda in the rhetorical style, chamber-music or no, of corresponding passages in the piano sonatas.

In the earliest surviving works it is the scherzos which seem the most characteristic and convincing movements, a fact which the Schumann circle probably recognised, since it was a scherzo which Brahms contributed in 1853 to the 'committee' sonata which Schumann organised as a surprise present to mark a visit of Joachim (see the *Sonatensatz*, p. 58). Though the influence of Beethoven is strong – how could it not be? – there is more than a hint in the 'weight' of the movements, their ample proportions, drastic rhythms and bold modulations of the highly individual free-standing scherzos of Chopin. In particular, Brahms's separate Scherzo for piano in E flat minor (typical key!), Op. 4, sounds at times like a gruff and powerful conflation of Chopin's scherzos in C sharp minor and B flat minor. The horn-calls which seem part and parcel of Brahms in this mood recur, though mainly at a distance, *staccato*, in the Trio's scherzo. The first *fortissimo* interrupts a shadowy cadence with a crash, and the vehement modulatory working-out is much more taut than anything else in this version of the work. The major-key tune of the 'trio' section is twice cunningly foreshadowed, first *pianissimo* on the violin over the piano's ever more fitful rhythms, then as a momentary counterpoint, first on the violin, then on the piano, to the scherzo's main horn-like theme. With the slower central 'trio' there returns the ardour and diatonic expansiveness which characterised so much of the first movement. There is a complete recapitulation followed by a striking, though not particularly integrated, coda in which the strings play ever-softer *pizzicato* cross-rhythms before ending on an off-beat chord to which they contribute an F sharp in three octaves.

Not many of Brahms's later works have a main theme which could be called picturesque, but the chorale-like first subject of this *adagio* is a candidate, being delivered by the piano with soft pedal down and hands wide apart, with the strings first confined to expressive interludes between the 'lines' of the chorale and only joining into the main fabric to help the rich but distant harmonies of the last line. The secondary theme is Schubertian, not only in its unconscious but glaring reminiscence of 'Am Meer' from the *Schwanengesang*, but also in the elongation of the first phrase from four bars to five by an ornamental echo.

Ex. 27

Schubert's *accompaniment* of his theme, though Brahms does not use it at this point, is a texture which comes all through Brahms's work – frequently in the first movement of this trio, for instance – and consists of the underlining of the theme with low-lying, and often doubled, parallel thirds, a Schubertian trait which prolonged usage makes us call Brahmsian. The reprise is marked by a spectacular modulation of one of the chorale 'lines', and is interrupted by an *allegro* of only marginal relevance. The strings contribute the same three F sharps to the soft final chord as they did to the end of the scherzo, making a curious but effective momentary integration.

The finale swings back to B minor, so that the four movements maintain the same tonic in a consistent major-minor alternation. Its first theme, though curiously interrupted by three *ritenuti* in succession, achieves a quiet momentum with its insistent rhythm. After a loud preparation, which perhaps 'protests too much' in its posturing, the cello announces a suave theme in six-bar phrases:

Ex. 28

Gal's surmise that this subject 'may derive from an unpublished song' is near the mark. It is in fact a pretty explicit reference to the last song of Beethoven's song-cycle *An die ferne Geliebte* ('To the distant beloved'): 'Nimm sie hin denn, diese Lieder' ('Take then these my songs'). In this case one could call it a quotation of a quotation, since it is this phrase which haunts the first movement of Schumann's great C major Fantasy for piano, Op. 17, a movement which Schumann described to Clara Wieck in their anguished separation before their marriage as 'a deep lament for you'. The subsequent tragedy of Schumann's madness, and Brahms's own relationship with Clara, might well have caused Brahms to regard the quotation in his trio as an unbearable reminder, let alone a formal misfit. After this Brahms employs a device he was later to use more purposefully – a 'premature' reprise in the tonic, followed by further development and a resumption, at its climax, of the recapitulation.

PIANO TRIO NO. I IN B, OP. 8 (SECOND VERSION, 1891)

Allegro con brio: Scherzo (Allegro molto): Adagio: Allegro.

For all its late date and wholesale revision, this second version can still in a sense be regarded as the first trio in the canon of Brahms's chamber music since, whilst pouncing like a hawk on the slightest inadequacies of technical detail, he yet had the instinctive tact and affection to retain all he could of the youthful themes in the tightening-up process, perhaps cherishing their warmth and impetuosity as evidences of a fire which he must sometimes have felt, in 1891, to have been reduced to a slow-burning glimmer.

The opening theme is quoted in the study of the first version (Ex. 24(i), p. 41) and Brahms permits it its full expanse of some sixty bars before turning vigorously aside to the relative minor key, in the process introducing triplets which from this point onwards are never far away, and which indeed dominate large sections subsequently. The secondary theme itself has a unison head and a harmonic tail, a tail whose dotted rhythms also contrast with the plain crotchets of the head. So deftly is the join made that it is hard to realise the passage of thirty-seven years in thirteen bars of transition, so to speak. The succinct variety of the new material lends itself to an easy extension to the double-bar, using cross-bar rhythms, a powerful restatement on the strings two octaves apart, and a reintroduction of the triplets. After a moment of meditative stillness the development never looks back but storms through a wide range of modulations whilst fusing first and second subjects. A striking and climactic equilibrium is achieved when the violin and cello play, literally in unison, a reprise of the first subject, which begins in the 'second-subject' key of the relative minor and then reverts in euphonious part-writing to the recapitulation in its 'proper' key. Nor is there any tired economy about the coda, which is tranquil and ample.

Except for tightening the coda Brahms has left the scherzo virtually unaltered, so that its paragraph in the description of the first version holds good. Brahms even retains, as befitting its exuberant style, the high octave *tremolando* at the climax of the 'Trio' in which the violin has to pretend to be the first and second violins of a symphony orchestra.

In the *adagio* the piano, with soft pedal down and hands well apart, takes over the final chord of the scherzo as the first of a chorale-like theme, between whose 'lines' the strings play interludes before joining in the rich soft harmonies of its conclusion. As in the first movement, Brahms chooses the relative minor for his second subject, and again there is a fruitful differentiation between its 'head', a wistful melody for cello whose phrase-length is made uneven by a Schubertian echo, and its 'tail', a typical pianistic combination of dotted-note sighs and rich low-lying interior harmonies. This motif is dovetailed into a reprise of the 'chorale' theme which is enhanced by a spectacular modulation to and from a far distance, and the movement ends with the same three F sharps on the strings as ended the scherzo.

The final *allegro* reverts to B minor, so that the four movements share the same tonic in symmetrical major/minor alternation. The quiet insistence of the main rhythm of the first subject: ♩ 𝄾 ♫ | ♩ ♩ is surprisingly broken by three *ritenuti* before a *fortissimo* sweeps it into the second theme, a square affair in D major with a heavy off-beat accompaniment for cello which is usually more notable for rosin than for anything else. Surprisingly, this paragraph comes to a quiet full-stop and there begins a recapitulation which though much varied in detail is a structural match of the exposition. It amounts to more than twenty bars

before it recollects itself, as it were, and plunges into developmental material until it is halted not by the first subject but by the
second in the major key. This in turn allows the first subject to
have the last, quite prolonged, say in the minor key, from which
it has never shown any sign of emerging.

The two versions compared
The detailed comparison is a lesson which no student composer
should deny himself, following the two scores side by side, note
by note. Short of this, however, there are several points which
the general reader may find interesting, ranging from large-scale
planning to tiny details.

It is the 'second-subject' paragraphs which are entirely recast.
A partly extra-musical reason has been advanced in the case of
the last movement, but in all three cases the cause of the dis-
satisfaction seems to lie in two overlapping considerations: the
paragraph seems to 'lose its way', lacking not only rhythmic
momentum but the sense of having a carefully considered
destination so far as key is concerned; and it is not, at the end of
the day, sufficiently integrated into the movement. Both considerations may be put in an unscientific nutshell: it doesn't
sound as if it belongs, as if it has to be thus and not otherwise.

That this part of the movement should be a crux for a young
composer in the mid-nineteenth century is a consequence of
Beethoven's achievements in transitions from first to second
paragraphs – not only in such awe-inspiring designs as the *Eroica*,
but also in such places as the first movement of the C minor
Piano Sonata, Op. 10, no. 1, or in its very close parallel in the
C minor String Quartet, Op. 18, no. 4. Mozart, on the contrary,
though there was nothing musically he could not do when he
gave his mind to it, could be content even in the *Jupiter* symphony
to use a rococo formula which in the post-*Eroica* light hardly
amounts to a transition at all. As Einstein has pointed out: 'If
all of Mozart's fragments of instrumental compositions should ever
become available in published form, it would be seen that most
of them break off before the development section . . . or during
it.'[1] Expositions, for him, were comparatively unproblematic.

Young Brahms is not of course ingenuous in his transitions;
he is merely ingenious where, especially after his splendid opening

[1] In *Mozart: his character, his work* (London 1947), p. 143.

phrases, ingenuity is not enough. For instance, in the first movement he isolates three descending quavers derived from the first
subject, elongates them, first in number and then in length of
notes, and finally painstakingly shows at the bottom of the texture
the relationship between the first subject and the second, underlining the portentousness of the preparation with a final *sostenuto*,
which for Brahms means *ritenuto*. His mature eye, as of a musical
plastic surgeon, enables him to make his reforming incision at
the very place where this preparation begins. The original ensuing
theme would have been insufficient even without a preparation
of this size; it resorts to a succession of piecemeal treatments
which do not culminate, and it hesitates between G♯ minor and
E major. Looked at dramatically, this sense of being at a loss,
only temporarily alleviated by a 'pastoral' excursion to the major,
may well have been exactly what Brahms intended after his
ebullient beginning. It would have been in keeping with contemporary compositional thought. All we can say is that it didn't
appeal to him a lifetime later.

With the slow movement the question of transition does not
arise, since the form is a simple ABA sandwich. But Brahms did
more than replace the too derivative secondary theme; he altered
its key from the subdominant E major to the relative minor
(G♯ minor). He may have felt that even in so still an *adagio* as this
the quietude, which is the inseparable effect of introducing the
subdominant (as opposed to the dominant) key, may have made
for too much languor. The change to the relative minor makes a
clearer change of mood but also matches the first movement's new
second paragraph, which replaced the previous indecision with an
unambiguous G♯ minor. He has thus brought about a much larger
long-range balance – the key centres of the first and third movements, as compared with those of the second and fourth, are: I, III:
B *major*, *down* through a minor third interval to G♯ minor; II, IV:
B *minor*, *up* through a minor third interval to D *major*.

The transition in the last movement, compared with its ultimate
form, is again rather vehement and lengthy, although it works
hard in its use of the dominating dotted rhythm of the main
subject, and also makes rhetorical play with a figure which turns
out to be the accompaniment of the 'Beethoven-quotation' tune.
This tune is a beautiful one in itself, but whether or not Brahms
would have suppressed it because it was derivative, it must have

seemed to him to be too lengthy and self-sufficient for a proper incorporation, as indeed the somewhat factitious effect of combining it with first-subject elements seems to show.

Having by the end of the exposition substantially different premisses on which to base further argument, it follows that Brahms's developments differ too widely for generalised discussion. What is clear is that the first version contains a succession of developmental treatments which can hardly escape sounding sectional (though ingenious) in spite of their persistent transformations and redecorations of the main theme, whereas in the second version far more diverse but shorter elements are welded into a whole which goes further (so far as modulation and textural and emotional variety are concerned) in a shorter time. The three early piano sonatas, as indeed Schubert's epoch-making *Wanderer-Fantasy* suggested, already show a proclivity towards a Lisztian thematic metamorphosis and interchange, not only within movements but from one movement to another. In Op. 1 the first subject renders the first movement almost monothematic, for all its wide divergencies of mood, and reappears transformed as the main subject of the finale; in Op. 2 the first fourteen bars of the slow movement are similarly transformed for the scherzo; in Op. 5 the first movement is almost as monothematic as in Op. 1, whilst the slow movement is deliberately recalled in an additional movement, an Intermezzo subtitled 'Rückblick' (backward glance). We know next to nothing that is trustworthy – and certainly nothing from Brahms – about the visit he made to Liszt before meeting Schumann; and if we disregard, as we must in this context, what Brahms later wrote about Liszt, we have nothing before us, certainly no instrumental works before this Op. 8 (except perhaps the scherzo, Op. 4) by which we could be certain that Brahms was not to follow his own version of a path trodden by Liszt and others which after all produced valid masterpieces. The fact remains that the first movement of the first version of Op. 8 is the last occasion on which Brahms in 'sonata-form' movements treats his main subject as the hero of a drama, the interest of whose plot lies in his constantly changing circumstances and the guises in which he meets them. A turning-point indeed, if so. But whether this rethinking was truly a volte-face or merely an instinctive conviction which the problems of large-scale composition brought to the forefront of consciousness, the crisis was past by the time of the orchestral Serenades, Opp. 11 and 16, and certainly shows no trace in the next chamber work, the Sextet in B flat, Op. 18. The other large-scale surgeries in Op. 8 follow inevitably from this rethinking – for example, the omission from the first movement's recapitulation of forty-one bars of ingenious *fugato*, followed by a dozen bars of fanfare (to greet its end?), the omission of a long *allegro* of doubtful provenance and motivation from the slow movement, and a drastic remodelling of the ends of the scherzo and last movement, making them less 'interesting' but more coherent.

Many of the minor alterations make the instrumental parts clearer and more telling (the piano part is even, very occasionally, slightly easier), but in this connection it is interesting to see what is left out of an otherwise salvaged passage: for instance, the violin's opening commentary on the cello's theme, discarded because it is merely, and obtrusively, ornamental. The word 'Finale' is probably dropped because by 1891 the word for Brahms seems to have had implications far removed from this movement's turbulent agitation. The change, in the first movement, from *allegro con moto* (1854) to *allegro con brio* (1891), with its impatience to be 'getting on with it', ought to have significance for those conductors who reserve a special kind of slow *allegro* for Brahms (but of course it won't).

PIANO TRIO NO. 2 IN C, OP. 87

Allegro: Andante con moto: Scherzo (Presto): Finale (Allegro giocoso).

The Olympian connotations of the key of C, building on the natural sonorities of the bottom note of the cello, are borne out in the mellow expansiveness of the first movement and especially in the broad sweep of its main theme, announced at both its initial appearances by the strings in octaves. Indeed, such is the exuberance and harmonic richness of the piano part that the strings are given simultaneous rhythms for much of the movement's course, often in octaves, as though in the face of the piano they heeded the maxim 'divided we fall'. Their first really separate voices are heard in an elegant phrase which winds downward to lead into the second subject group – the counterpart of the similar phrase which winds upwards with the same purpose in the Violin Concerto. This subject-group has a variety of phrase, rhythm, texture and incidental modulation which betokens the highest imaginative power, and the flowing but rapid sequence of at least four strongly characterised themes has an almost Mozartian profusion about it. What is more, although each theme begins with a four-bar phrase, in none of the four cases does the answering phrase amount to four bars. Thus what would be a mere catalogue in verbal description is not even a procession in aural effect, but an irresistible ride which cannot be ended until the last of the paragraph has been heard. When at length this moment has come we are punctually transplanted to our original C and our opening theme. This, however, as fairly often, turns out to be a feint, and we embark on a development which clearly cannot lack material. In the circumstances quite a surprising time is allotted to an elongation of the main subject in one of the few string dialogues. The recapitulation is perfectly regular, and a sizeable coda is begun with another reference to the string dialogue which thus formally explains itself.

The second movement is a theme and five variations, again rich in detail and wide-ranging in style, but like all Brahms's variations rigorous in their basic relationship to their original. A case in point is the last seven bars of the theme which consist of a four-bar phrase and its inversion telescoped thus:

For four variations the concluding seven bars, though varying widely in actual melody, all adhere strictly to this seven-bar-with-inversion pattern. Put like this it sounds merely academic; in effect it is this meticulous bone-structure which enables us to enjoy the flesh, as also the effect in the last variation when the seven-bar prison is broken and the music expands lovingly to its dying fall.

The main limb of the scherzo is, except for one outburst in a distant key, an affair of fleeting shadows requiring great agility, from the pianist especially. The centre section comes out into the light of day with a diatonic tune.

When Brahms from time to time writes the word 'finale' it is as though he gives notice to the world that he is stripped for action of a more rhythmical, less introspective sort. Here the two sides of Brahms's creativity are happily in balance. On the one hand a profuse and speedy outpouring of several themes, diverse both in their initial character and in their modulations and twists of rhythm; on the other hand a stealthy, witty form of elaborating them so that as the party proceeds we realise we are at a family party.

PIANO TRIO NO. 3 IN C MINOR, OP. 101[1]

Allegro energico: Presto non assai: Andante grazioso: Allegro molto.

The first movement deploys themes which are well differentiated but not notably different from Brahms's usual 'fierce' ones. The *legato* conjunct rise of the second subject allies it to many such. The interest lies in their development, which begins with a combination of both subjects, the triplet figure from the first throwing a constantly new light. The development is short, not discursive, and leads to a recapitulation, not of the first theme (which is not swallowed up *en passant*; it simply isn't there), but of a passage which was originally a pendant to it. The first theme later climaxes the movement, whose final bars contain some unusual and powerful octaves between top and bottom, reminiscent of late Schubert songs such as 'Der Atlas'.

The second movement reverts to the shadowy minor-key genre of the intermezzo of the first Piano Quartet, but here it is more succinct and straightforward in form. The next movement initially patterns its phrases in units of seven beats made up of a 3/4 followed by two bars of 2/4. The symmetrical asymmetry characteristically broadens to phrases of ten crotchets plus four at the cadence. The strings (without benefit of sustaining pedal) are allotted phrases each of which the piano subsequently shows how to perform. The central section is more animated, in mainly five-beat phrases. The reprise has a rearranged and more whimsical distribution between piano and strings, though still, one feels, to the latter's disadvantage.

The final movement is again succinct, so much so as to call in question the idea of the consoling and solidifying major version

[1] A Piano Trio in A published by Breitkopf in 1938 can safely be regarded as spurious.

of the main theme – an apotheosis insufficiently prepared? Brahms made this interesting comment on it to Elisabeth von Herzogenberg: 'I should think the Trio's finale requires, first very careful handling, then the reverse!'

TRIO FOR PIANO, VIOLIN AND HORN IN E FLAT, OP. 40

Andante, alternating with *Poco più animato: Scherzo (Allegro): Adagio mesto: Finale (Allegro con brio).*

Apart from its unusual instrumental combination this work is unique in the chamber works in not having a sonata-form opening movement. The woodland associations of the horn lead Brahms to a meditative lyricism unsuitable to questing drama, and the first two *andante* paragraphs begin and end in the home key – the antithesis of sonata procedures. These *andante* paragraphs alternate with slightly faster sections in the minor key, which however are not so dramatic as to overbalance the pastoral musing, and the final *andante* in contrast to its previous conservativeness enhances the ecstatic effect by beginning in a far-away key *pianissimo* – truly an echo of an echo, coming home by a long unfolding of melody and modulation.

The more robust side of the horn is reflected in the ample scherzo, whose much slower middle section in seven flats (Ab minor) presages the rapt and doleful slow movement. This in turn pre-echoes, as in a distant slow fanfare (bars 59–60) the main subject of the finale, which gives free range, in 6/8 time and ample sonata form, to the hunting instincts of the horn.

Duos

SONATA FOR PIANO AND VIOLIN NO. 1 IN G, OP. 78

Vivace ma non troppo: Adagio: Allegro molto moderato.

Considering that the most frequent duo in chamber music is violin and piano, it is remarkable that there are only three sonatas and that the first did not appear till 1880. Perhaps this is again a case of hesitating to tread classical ground. Brahms's sense of tradition extends to the old-fashioned usage – also in the cello sonatas – of putting the piano first in the titles. The labours and experience of the Violin Concerto, composed more or less contemporaneously, may well have cleared the way. Certainly this first movement represents a high point in which, to an extent rare in his predecessors including Beethoven, Brahms deploys the natural *cantabile* of the violin and the natural but quite different sonorities of the piano so perfectly, and in the service of such beautiful material, that good players experience a physical as well as an aural pleasure in their performance. Often in Brahms the feeling of struggle is part and parcel of the music itself – not that the music is badly written. But here the limpid, perfectly-balanced texture and the gentle but irresistible flow of varied but cognate ideas, make for an Apollonian experience quite out of the ordinary. The characteristic cross-rhythm and rest (*Atempause*) of the Viennese waltz (♩ ♪ ♪ ♩) haunts the music from its first bar – as it haunted the violinist-turned-composer Sibelius in his violin concerto and elsewhere. With the rests removed (♩ ♩. ♪ ♩) it begins both the subsidiary subjects. A typical new-wine-in-old-bottles effect is made at bar 82. Here the music settles into the home key and first subject, as though we had reached the orthodox double-bar and were repeating the exposition. We know this cannot literally be so, for we are hearing *pizzicato* for the first time whilst the piano plays the first subject. But the music is very leisurely about diverging into development. A similar process of pseudo-repeat comes in the first movement of the Fourth Symphony. Another beauty, at once intellectual and sensuous, is the recapitulation itself. Twice the violin starts the subject, but the piano harmonies are still preparatory. A few bars later the original tempo is resumed and we are truly home, but starting in the second bar of the theme. The effect is of arriving at some beloved spot and being met by friends who share our surprise that the train is a few minutes early.

The key of the slow movement, E flat, added to the lyricism of the first, lends some colour to Kalbeck's comparison of this sonata to Beethoven's last violin sonata. In spite of the sophisticated figuration with which the violin's song is clothed, this is basically a simple shape (ABABA). In the 'B' of the design the *Atempause* recurs, but now more in the manner of a funeral march.

The main subject of the last movement and its pattering accompaniment is based on a song called 'Regenlied' (Rain-song) published in 1873 as Op. 59, no. 3. The words may be paraphrased: 'Awake my childhood dream again, O rain. . . . Arouse my old songs again.' This nostalgia for the refreshment of being bedewed, like a new baptism, must have been influential with Brahms, for he reverted to it in one of his finest songs, 'Sapphic Ode', whose refrains equated the dew of kisses and the dew of tears. This last movement begins with the *Atempause* (here ♪♫ | ♩) yet again, and the rhythm is never far away. Formally the music has a surprise in store. The 'rain' theme gives way to a more whimsical theme with a momentary stop to the piano's shower of semiquavers. The first movement may have put us on our guard against deceptive reprises, but a literal repeat of the main theme prepares us for a rondo shape. Surprisingly the next episode is quotation, and wide-ranging development, of the theme of the second movement; this gives way to the return of the 'rain', but when at last the home major key is heard (for the first time since the first movement) this *adagio* theme again suffuses the texture, and the quiet and beautiful close contains more than a hint of the first movement's harmonies as well as the by now omnipresent *Atempause*.

SONATA FOR PIANO AND VIOLIN NO. 2 IN A, OP. 100

Allegro amabile: Andante tranquillo, alternating with *Vivace: Allegretto grazioso (quasi andante).*

This work, written in a flower-laden villa by the lake of Thun in the summer of 1886, has, as Brahms says, a number of songs 'going with the sonata'. Two of the songs, 'Wie Melodien' and 'Immer leiser wird mein Schlummer' (written before but published after the sonata), were sung there on a tender visit made by the soprano Hermine Spies. The second subject is an adaptation of the opening of 'Wie Melodien', whose words liken love to imagined melody, to transient wafts of scented flowers. The climax of 'Immer leiser' is at the words 'Komm', O komme bald, (Come soon), and uses the rising-third phrase with which the third movement begins. There is also a song called 'Komm bald, which puts the request more tenderly: 'Why wait from day to day? All the garden is blooming for you to see', and this song is entwined in the first movement.[1] These threads, taken with the *amabile*, all seem to hang together.

The sonata begins with a good example of Brahms's regular irregularity, a whole series of five-bar phrases caused by each instrument adding a one-bar echo[2] to his partner's four-bar phrases. More important structurally than the 'Wie Melodien' second subject is the next theme

Ex. 29

whose repeated notes, lengthened to ♩ ♩, play a prominent part in the anchors which the music throws out as it enters port.

The second-movement sandwich is the familiar one of slow movement and scherzo elements, but it contains subtle contrasts in their treatment. If we discount the brief throw-away *vivace* at the end, the two other 'scherzo' passages are identical, bar for bar, in structure, harmony and key, but the second moves faster and forms a strict variation of the first, using *pizzicato* and syncopation freely. Each *andante* arranges a melody (which at first hearing seems indivisible) in different ways and keys, fluctuating between the twin poles of the movement, F (major) and D (major and minor), whose outcome is in doubt till the end.

The lyrical but formally unconventional last movement almost pointedly avoids the usual last-movement attributes, unless one can persuade oneself that one is listening to a rondo of sorts. The listener will hear for himself the point of structure which most puzzled Brahms's friends: after the opening thirty bars of flowing tune the music enters upon a passage whose rhythms and harmonies are clouded with piano arpeggios: it sounds like a transition preparing for a 'second-subject' tune; suddenly we slip back to the home key and the main tune and are left to suppose that the 'cloud' passage is not a transition (since transitions lead somewhere) but an event in itself – a 'subject'. The weightiest episode is yet to come, an almost impulsive melody in a minor

[1] Gal follows Brahms's biographer Kalbeck in seeing a quotation from a fourth song, 'Am Kirchhofe', in the last movement, but this is more dubious.

[2] The first 'echo' turns out to be the second bar of the second subject.

key which occupies the middle of the movement and which returns more placidly in a coda which is warm rather than demonstrative, but which, taken together with the pervasive lyricism of the whole work, stimulated Elisabeth von Herzogenberg to say 'the whole sonata is one caress'.

SONATA FOR PIANO AND VIOLIN NO. 3 IN D MINOR, OP. 108

Allegro: Adagio: Un poco presto e con sentimento: Presto agitato.

This last violin sonata, dedicated to the conductor Hans von Bülow, is bigger than the other two, not only in having an extra movement but because the ideas, at least in the outer movements, have a more compelling sweep altogether. Although the tense opening page is marked *sotto voce*, the restless piano syncopations and the two-in-a-bar unequivocal *allegro* ensure that undertones of drama immediately tinge the violin's song, and it is not long before the first *forte* breaks out. The movement is tautly constructed: for instance the transition motif (bars 40–42) serves also within the second-subject paragraph as both episode (bars 56 ff.) and coda (bars 74 ff.), where it is divided between violin and piano and typically elongated. The 'development' is a *tour de force:* it is 46 bars of *sotto voce* discussion of the first subject, all delivered over the note A struck like a soft, insistent drum-beat on all 184 crotchets. The same technique, on D, is used to make a balancing coda.

The same taut construction goes into the slow movement and makes it sound like a long seamless melody, in which the two bars of upward-winding semiquavers (bars 19–20, 51–2) are reminiscent of the Violin Concerto.

Though the third movement is the lightest in style and begins as if it aims at no more than an airy intermezzo, it soon begins to attach more weight to its falling thirds which generate an energetic passage in a distant key. The hesitant and mock-sorrowful modulation back gives a witty impression of apology for having gone too far.

If the previous finales of violin sonatas have avoided the issue of culmination, this one flings itself straight into a forceful gallop, to which the nearest approach in the mature chamber music is the finale of the Horn Trio, though the movement in its combination of grim 6/8 dance with chorale-style second subject also evokes the finale of the early Piano Sonata in F minor, Op. 5. The violin is even denied its cantabile at the opening, but throws itself into a fierce accompaniment à la Beethoven. At the end of the exposition we have a pseudo-repeat of the opening, which collapses into a development section notable for its ever more insistent syncopations. But even after this excitement the control is unrelenting – the recapitulation is taken up not at the beginning, but at the very point where it was broken off 64 bars before. The last page, as it storms home in the minor with a glint of major, recaptures on the piano the virtuoso writing with which Brahms the young eagle swooped on Schumann so many years before.

SONATENSATZ (SCHERZO) FOR VIOLIN AND PIANO

This was written in 1853 as young Brahms's contribution to a committee sonata written as a surprise greeting for Joachim on his arrival at Düsseldorf for a concert with Schumann. Schumann wrote the second and fourth movements and Albert Dietrich the first.[1] This scherzo (6/8 time, C minor) pounds along in unmistakable style, though the violin sometimes has an unequal struggle on its hands. The trio reads like an affectionate parody of Schumann's style, a compliment suitable enough for the composer of 'Chopin'.

SONATA FOR PIANO AND CELLO NO. I IN E MINOR, OP. 38

Allegro non troppo: Allegretto quasi Menuetto: Allegro.
(There was originally an *adagio* too, but Brahms removed it.)

Brahms indulges his penchant for the richer and more sombre instrumental colours by his choice of the cello for his first duo sonata, which in spite of the intermittent beauties of Chopin's and Mendelssohn's contributions is unquestionably the first important cello sonata since Beethoven. The leisurely unfolding

[1] Dietrich, in his memoirs, says, 'Brahms wrote the scherzo on a theme from my first movement. After having played the sonata with Clara Schumann, Joachim immediately recognised the author of each part.' Dietrich and Wildman, *Recollections of Johannes Brahms*, translated by Dora Hecht (London 1899), p. 5.

of the cello's theme, first on the bottom string and then on the top, to the accompaniment of off-beat sighing chords, is the epitome of the instrument's noble gravity. Equally effective are the other two main subjects, one robust in the minor key with characteristic cross-rhythm strivings between the partners, and the other a consolatory cadence-theme in the major. There is a fairly large proportion of non-melodic figuration as well, but the resulting gruffness is in character, both of composer and instrument.

Far removed from gruffness is the sad whimsicality of the second movement, which serves rather as intermezzo than centre-piece. The chief sophisticating element is the piano's 'lead-in' phrase which haunts the movement in various guises and which sometimes invades the other material. From it are also derived the hesitating phrases which punctuate the subdued passion of the otherwise perpetual motion of the trio.

With so few examples before him of cello sonatas of the first rank it is hardly surprising that Brahms is led by Beethoven's last cello sonata to embark upon a fugued final movement, if not a fugue as such. Geiringer has pointed out the subject's virtual identity with that of Contrapunctus 13 in Bach's *Art of Fugue* (though it is difficult to concede the close relationship he claims between Contrapunctus 3 and the main theme of the first movement). If Beethoven's fugue poses balance problems, those of the Brahms movement are notorious, the gruff triplets of the subject being difficult enough to enunciate on the cello without the enthusiastic collaboration of a pianist who tends to take by storm (if he takes at all) a succession of difficult trills, double thirds, and octaves. Until towards the end of the development the outlines of sonata form are clearly apparent, with a finely sustained fugal exposition corresponding to first subject, and with continuing imitative entries forming a transition to the secondary paragraph in the usual relative major. At this point what was the counter-subject flowers in varied forms into a 'secondary-subject' group. The turbulence of the main subject is soon resumed through a wide range of modulations. A hammered pedal-point both below and above the subject (somewhat in the manner of the fugue from the piano Variations on a Theme of Handel) retrieves the stability of key and is preparing us for a reprise, but surprisingly has a quiet dalliance with the 'second subject' again, a studied anticlimax which allows the first fugal subject to have the last word and to storm home in a *più presto* coda.

SONATA FOR PIANO AND CELLO NO. 2 IN F, OP. 99

Allegro vivace: Adagio affettuoso: Allegro passionato: Allegro molto.

This sonata employs a blander, higher range of the cello than the first, is more profuse and varied in its subject matter, wears its heart on its sleeve in a true *adagio*, and after a return to turbulence in the third movement adds a nonchalant fourth. Apart from the compulsively leaping first subject, much of the texture of the first movement is based on *tremolandi* for both partners, which in the piano's case develops into a nocturne-like central episode whose shadows, distant key and subtle syncopations make a striking contrast to the surrounding exuberance. As with the Fourth Symphony the recapitulation is marked by a soft return of the main subject in longer notes.

For a sonata in F the *adagio* adopts the very distant key of F sharp, the change making the effect of a new plane such as Orpheus might have felt in the Elysian fields. But equally surprising, the secondary theme, announced by the cello after only 19 bars, is back in F minor – of all unlikely and apparently inaccessible keys. Dramatic use is made of *pizzicato* in both low and high registers, a device not frequent in Brahms.

With the third movement Brahms reverts to the stormy style of his youth, but made more powerful by the prolonged *sotto voce* from which the explosions break out, and by a marked economy of motifs. The piano part is amongst his most taxing. It is interesting to note that the far more suave Trio again finds itself in F sharp at one point, having begun in F.

After three such movements, big in style and substantial in length, the last movement poses a puzzle because, at *allegro molto* and two in a bar, it seems to make a tailpiece so light as to be almost frivolous. It is a rondo whose brief episode of darker emotion with its sobbing rests gives a foretaste of *Pagliacci*, but could be more scientifically referred to the second subject of the slow movement.

Indian Summer - The Clarinet Works

The final flowering of Brahms's art, at a time when he had himself hinted that he had said his say, was stimulated by the artistry of the clarinettist Mühlfeld, whom Brahms had met in 1891. The four works that resulted share the sweet sadness which the clarinet, of all instruments, most powerfully evokes, and which because of Brahms's use of it must for ever be tinged with autumnal nostalgia. In the works themselves the tension generated by Brahms's mastery of economical motivic construction is the dominant trait – a tension allied with terseness which dominated the two last works of all, the Four Serious Songs and the eleven Chorale Preludes for organ. Of the Clarinet Quintet it seems paradoxical to speak of terseness when in the slow movement one experiences something of the timeless trance-like standing outside the world which is the literal meaning of ecstasy; yet even here the concentration into the still moment can only be achieved, without disrupting the formal whole, by the hard-won experience of a lifetime in the ceaseless struggle towards coherence between matter and manner.

TRIO FOR PIANO, CLARINET AND CELLO IN A MINOR, OP. 114

Allegro: Adagio: Andante grazioso: Allegro.

It may have been that in setting his composing pen to work again Brahms unconsciously reverted to comparatively recent ideas from his great stockpile. In his last orchestral work, the Double Concerto for violin and cello, Op. 102, he had three years previously faced the problem of matching a cello with an instrument likely to steal the limelight. In the Clarinet Trio, as in the concerto, we have not only the same keys of first and second movements, but also in its first paragraph a theme of which dotted rhythm and crotchet triplets are strong features; and this theme is immediately followed by one whose basic rhythm –

♩ |♩ ♩ ♩ ♩ |♪ etc. – has an obvious affinity with the second subject of the concerto. But whereas the concerto's use of the theme was on the whole joyous, even impetuous, the trio uses it almost entirely in the minor, and to an extent which permeates most of the movement, leaving the other second-group themes rather pale and episodic by comparison.

With three such instruments at command, to write a slow movement which did not exploit fantasy and passion in idio-syncratic terms would have been a wilful abdication. It is only after acknowledging this foremost pleasure that the listener if he wishes can turn to the score to note how Brahms's variation and extension techniques can achieve so great a range of expressiveness in a coherent terse whole of less than 60 bars. The terseness deepens, and throws into relief the magical moment of lingering, with the clarinet and cello gently languishing in octaves, which occurs midway in the reprise (bars 42–4). Yet the lingering is not the indulgence it might have been in Brahms's mid-career. It is paid for by a characteristic shortening of the recapitulation up to this point.

In the scherzo-substitute we have a paler but equally elegant re-creation of the mood of the *Liebeslieder* waltzes by a man who was still a Viennese, albeit a *fin-de-siècle*, knowing one. The mock-innocent start makes the subsequent dimensions a surprise.

In the last movement, as in the Double Concerto, the music reverts to the minor, and the cello keeps its end up by announcing both the principal themes, the latter of which whimsically varies with three-time bars the pounding duple rhythms of the rest of the movement. The listener following its form by ear may need to be warned that the first subject returns immediately after the exposi-tion as though for a repeat; the music then diverges into a swiftly modulating development, and when it returns to an even keel it takes up the real reprise exactly where the false reprise left it off, so that we don't formally hear the first subject again. Not that this matters, since by now the strong family likeness of both first and second themes has been made more explicit.

CLARINET QUINTET IN B MINOR, OP. 115

Allegro: Adagio: Andantino, leading into *Presto non assai, ma con sentimento: Con moto.*

It is only in the third bar that the opening theme, which could till then be heard as in D major, takes on its B minor colouring. This ambiguity becomes more pronounced in the third movement, and is one of the several unifying features in this closely integrated work.

Ex. 30

Note how at the clarinet's entry the strings are static and again in D major. With what delicious amplitude does the clarinet's opening fall on the ear, with the phrase marked *a* achieving a new dimension by its long notes taking one-and-a-half bars instead of half a bar! To demonstrate properly the mastery with which the procession of seemingly disparate themes in the exposition are related by subtle cross-references of shape and rhythm would mean quoting all 70 bars. But the first pendant to the main theme could be quoted both for its fastidious scoring and also for its use of phrase *b* from Ex. 30 as a new growth-point:

Ex. 31

But the whole score is full of cross-references, of which a few samples must suffice. Here, beginning on the F#, is the melody of the first vigorous chordal phrase for comparison with the first three bars of Ex. 30:

Ex. 32

This is the clarinet's beginning of the second subject group (for the same comparison on a smaller and more tenuous scale):

Ex. 33

The second violin's answer in Ex. 33 shortly afterwards heads a new melody which in fact uses both limbs of Ex. 33 and helps to end the exposition (note the new accidentals):

Ex. 34

The development falls into two strongly contrasted parts: in the first the plaintive semiquavers of Ex. 30 permeate a passage of sustained energy; in the second there is a compensating contrast when, in a slightly slower tempo, the formerly vigorous Ex. 32 grows ever more contemplative until at the resumption of the original tempo phrase *b* in its most melting variant precipitates the recapitulation.

In the *adagio* the quintessence of romanticism lies in the melody hovering over the muted strings, which support it with syncopations and twos-against-threes, whose object is not an assertion of rhythms but a yearning undulation from which melodic shapes emerge as though the emotion of the moment compels them to articulateness. The main melodic shape,

Ex. 35

though not alluded to in any explicit way in the first movement, seems to be implicit. Perhaps it is a rearrangement of the intervals in phrase *b*, but one makes such anachronistic analysis at one's peril, and can readily imagine the composer's contemptuous rejoinder. Just before the rhapsodic *più lento* of the central section of the movement the main phrase, by the addition of one note, makes four-beat phrases extend across the three-beat bars:

Ex. 36

The lead into the *più lento* is, however, an explicit reference to the first theme of the Quintet, though its first bar (bar 42) with F♯ on the clarinet and D and C♯ on the viola also ties it in with the *adagio*'s subject. This same shape is the basic one of the *più lento*, where the clarinet has a seeming Hungarian rhapsody whilst the *tremolandi* of the strings lend intermittent shudders to the texture, as though imitating the cimbalom. But again we meet the Brahmsian paradox; the elaborate roulades, the (for Brahms) vertiginous extremes of compass turn out to be held in a close formal grip. Most of the clarinet's rhapsodising is in four-in-a-bar, in contrast to which the appearance by way of coda (bar 128) of the same material smoothed out into triplets in the prevailing triple time makes an effect of blissful calm.

The calm is not much modified by the third movement, the beginning of which, at any rate, seems to be the extreme point in the reaction away from the traditional scherzo. The tune itself seems to be making a point of being like the first movement, being conjunct and veering between D and B minor. It is as though Brahms was intent on remaining in a chiaroscuro world, as a painter might be who was obsessed with autumn tints. But the *andantino* stops and gives way to a *presto non assai* (in B minor, by way of a change!). Its subject is obviously derived from the first four notes of the *andantino*, enlivened with repeated notes and dotted rhythms, and by a witty stroke it is accompanied by another figure from the *andantino* (from bars 19–20). This slower/faster relationship of the same material reminds the listener at first of the similar sandwich in the third movement of the Second Symphony, but this faster section turns out to be a sonata form in its own right which does not return to the original tempo but which does, characteristically and in spite of its B minor home key, end in D major with the same lingering cadence which ended the *andantino*.

After three such integrated movements we might expect a finale to explode into at any rate an initial animated contrast. What does Brahms give us? A conjunct tune, marked no more than *con moto*, in B minor with conspicuous touches of D major! This is the subject of five variations, the last of which, being in triple time, enables the music to revert by way of nostalgic coda to the material of the first movement. The effect is in marked contrast to the sometimes contrived effect of cyclic procedures, since it is the logical conclusion in a literal sense of the under-lying integrities of the whole work. The nostalgia has an ache to it, the second note of the B minor scale being sometimes flattened to C natural as though it had lost the energy to raise itself further.

SONATA FOR CLARINET (OR VIOLA) AND PIANO IN F MINOR, OP. 120, NO. 1

Allegro appassionato: Andante un poco adagio: Allegretto grazioso: Vivace.

Again Brahms entering on a new genre, even late in life, begins in a minor key. One cannot in the face of his *appassionato* talk of 'all passion spent', but it is smouldering rather than explosive, and the economy of some of the writing, with age reinforcing his predisposition not to write two notes where one will do, lends the music a rather gaunt austerity, especially in the opening. Though the motifs of the exposition each enter as new persons, their interrelationships are subtly unfolded as the music proceeds. The *sostenuto ed espressivo* of the coda summarises the movement in concentrated emotion, and yet even here it is still growing out of earlier material.

In the *andante* the gentle roulades have a vein of characteristic fantasy. Though the sonata shape is just discernible the closely integrated motivic work balances the wide-ranging harmonies to give the impression of a continuous nocturne-like song.

The main mood of the next short movement is like a gentle Ländler. Its contrasting middle section is Brahms's last visit to F minor, the key which ever since the early Piano Sonata, Op. 5, evoked turbulent passion. Here at last it is sweetly plaintive, with exploitation of the clarinet's bottom notes.

The last movement is a cheerful, mainly extravert rondo (ABACBA). The limb represented by C in this scheme is in the minor; considering how closely knit the rest of the sonata is, it stands curiously apart, perhaps in deliberate contrast to the otherwise omnipresent motif of three repeated notes.

SONATA FOR CLARINET (OR VIOLA) AND PIANO IN E FLAT, OP. 120, NO. 2

Allegro amabile: Allegro appassionato: Andante con moto, with final *allegro.*

With this first movement Brahms consummates his mastery of the plastic variation of his material, both in melody and accompaniment, so that innumerable cross-references integrate the whole, though not obtrusively since the general effect is of unbroken song. (Many are the clarinettists who joy in the *amabile* and who ignore the *allegro.*)

Some aspects of the second movement point to it as the last of the scherzo-substitutes: its triple rhythm, its fairly simple ternary shape, and the final appearance in Brahms's works of the sostenuto big tune largely in thirds and sixths by way of 'Trio'. Yet it is more of a centrepiece, a passionate counterpoise to the suavity of the first movement and the relaxed charm of the final movement.

This is a set of variations whose shapely tune begins with formal symmetry, but which typically ends with a six-bar rather than a four- or eight-bar phrase. Brahms for the first three variations uses the old technique of successively shortening the ruling note-lengths. After a variation of dreamy syncopated chords and another forming a minor-key *allegro,* the tailpiece of the main tune moves to the centre of the stage before the final short burst of rhythmic energy brings this unique corpus of chamber music to a close.

Index of Works